First World War
and Army of Occupation
War Diary
France, Belgium and Germany

3 CAVALRY DIVISION
Divisional Troops
12 Sanitary Section
11 January 1915 - 30 June 1917

WO95/1149/1

The Naval & Military Press Ltd
www.nmarchive.com
Published in association with The National Archives

Published by

The Naval & Military Press Ltd

Unit 10 Ridgewood Industrial Park,

Uckfield, East Sussex,

TN22 5QE England

Tel: +44 (0) 1825 749494

www.naval-military-press.com

www.nmarchive.com

This diary has been reprinted in facsimile from the original. Any imperfections are inevitably reproduced and the quality may fall short of modern type and cartographic standards.

© Crown Copyright
Images reproduced by permission of The National Archives, London, England, 2015.

Contents

Document type	Place/Title	Date From	Date To
Heading	WO95/1149/1		
Heading	B.E.F. France & Flanders. 3 Cavalry Div. Troops. 12 Sanitary Section. 1915 Jan To 1917 June. 13 Mobile Veterinary Section. 1914 Oct To 1919 Apr. 14 Mob Veterinary Section. 1914 Oct To 1919 May. 20 Mob Veterinary Section. 1915 Mar To 1918 Feb.		
Heading	No. 12 Sanitary Section Jan 1915-June 1917		
Heading	No 12. Sanitary Section 3rd Cavy Division Vol I Jan 1915-Dec 1916		
War Diary	Morbecque	11/01/1915	11/01/1915
War Diary	Starbeeke	11/01/1915	11/01/1915
War Diary	Morbecque	12/01/1915	12/01/1915
War Diary	Hazebrouck	12/01/1915	12/01/1915
War Diary	Morbecque	13/01/1915	13/01/1915
War Diary	Hondeghem	14/01/1915	14/01/1915
War Diary	Morbecque	14/01/1915	15/01/1915
War Diary	Hazebrouck	16/01/1915	16/01/1915
War Diary	Hondeghem	18/01/1915	23/01/1915
War Diary	Vieux Berquin	25/01/1915	25/01/1915
War Diary	Hazebrouck	25/01/1915	25/01/1915
War Diary	Handeghem	25/01/1915	25/01/1915
War Diary	Hazebrouck	26/01/1915	26/01/1915
War Diary	Handeghem	26/01/1915	26/01/1915
War Diary	Hazebrouck	27/01/1915	31/01/1915
Heading	No. 12. Sanitary Section 3rd Cavalry Division Vol II		
War Diary	Hazebrouck	01/02/1915	05/02/1915
War Diary	Ypres	06/02/1915	12/02/1915
War Diary	Hazeb'k	13/02/1915	17/02/1915
War Diary	Hazebrouck	18/02/1915	28/02/1915
Heading	No 12. Sanitary Section. 3rd Cavalry Division Vol III		
War Diary	Hazebrouck	01/03/1915	01/03/1915
War Diary	Hondeghem	01/03/1915	01/03/1915
War Diary	Ebblinghem	02/03/1915	03/03/1915
War Diary	Hazebrouck	03/03/1915	04/03/1915
War Diary	Steenbecque	04/03/1915	04/03/1915
War Diary	Ebblinghem	04/03/1915	04/03/1915
War Diary	Hazebrouck	04/03/1915	05/03/1915
War Diary	Steenbecque	06/03/1915	06/03/1915
War Diary	Hazebrouck	07/03/1915	17/03/1915
War Diary	Sercus	17/03/1915	17/03/1915
War Diary	Hazebrouck	17/03/1915	19/03/1915
War Diary	Boeseghem	20/03/1915	20/03/1915
War Diary	Hazebrouck	21/03/1915	22/03/1915
War Diary	Ebblinghem	23/03/1915	23/03/1915
War Diary	Hazebrouck	23/03/1915	28/03/1915
War Diary	Hondeghem	29/03/1915	31/03/1915
War Diary	Steenbecque	31/03/1915	31/03/1915
War Diary	Hazebrouck	31/03/1915	31/03/1915
Heading	No. 12 Sany: Section 3rd Cav: Division Vol IV		
War Diary	Hazebrouck	01/04/1915	01/04/1915

War Diary	Ebblinghem Hazebrouck	02/04/1915	05/04/1915
War Diary	Morbecque	06/04/1915	07/04/1915
War Diary	Hazebrouck	07/04/1915	07/04/1915
War Diary	Morbecque	08/04/1915	08/04/1915
War Diary	Hazebrouck	08/04/1915	08/04/1915
War Diary	Sercus	09/04/1915	10/04/1915
War Diary	Hazebrouck	10/04/1915	11/04/1915
War Diary	Morbecque	12/04/1915	12/04/1915
War Diary	Lynde	13/04/1915	13/04/1915
War Diary	Renescure	13/04/1915	13/04/1915
War Diary	Morbecque	14/04/1915	14/04/1915
War Diary	Hazebrouck	14/04/1915	14/04/1915
War Diary	Lynde	15/04/1915	15/04/1915
War Diary	Sercus	15/04/1915	15/04/1915
War Diary	Hazebrouck	16/04/1915	16/04/1915
War Diary	Lynde	16/04/1915	17/04/1915
War Diary	Hazebrouck	17/04/1915	17/04/1915
War Diary	Steenbecque	18/04/1915	18/04/1915
War Diary	Lynde	18/04/1915	18/04/1915
War Diary	Steenbecque	19/04/1915	19/04/1915
War Diary	Lynde	19/04/1915	20/04/1915
War Diary	Hazebrouck	20/04/1915	21/04/1915
War Diary	Lynde	21/04/1915	21/04/1915
War Diary	Wallon Cappel	22/04/1915	22/04/1915
War Diary	Hazebrouck	22/04/1915	28/04/1915
War Diary	Morbecque	28/04/1915	29/04/1915
War Diary	Hazebrouck	29/04/1915	30/04/1915
Heading	No 12. Sanitary Section Vol V		
War Diary	Hazebrouck	01/05/1915	18/05/1915
War Diary	Point 35	18/05/1915	18/05/1915
War Diary	Hazebrouck	19/05/1915	19/05/1915
War Diary	Point 35.	19/05/1915	22/05/1915
War Diary	Hazebrouck	23/05/1915	26/05/1915
War Diary	Renescure	27/05/1915	27/05/1915
War Diary	Hazebrouck	27/05/1915	27/05/1915
War Diary	Renescure	28/05/1915	29/05/1915
War Diary	Vlamertinghe	30/05/1915	31/05/1915
Heading	No. 12. Sanitary Section 3rd Cavalry Division Vol VI		
War Diary	Vlamertinghe	01/06/1915	01/06/1915
War Diary	Ypres	01/06/1915	01/06/1915
War Diary	Campayne	01/06/1915	01/06/1915
War Diary	Hazebrouck	01/06/1915	02/06/1915
War Diary	Ypres	02/06/1915	02/06/1915
War Diary	Vlamertinghe	02/06/1915	02/06/1915
War Diary	Hazebrouck	02/06/1915	02/06/1915
War Diary	Campayne	02/06/1915	02/06/1915
War Diary	Vlamertinghe	03/06/1915	03/06/1915
War Diary	Ypres	03/06/1915	03/06/1915
War Diary	Hazebrouck	03/06/1915	03/06/1915
War Diary	Vlamertinghe	04/06/1915	04/06/1915
War Diary	Renescure	04/06/1915	04/06/1915
War Diary	Hazebrouck	04/06/1915	05/06/1915
War Diary	Vlamertinghe	05/06/1915	05/06/1915
War Diary	Hazebrouck	06/06/1915	06/06/1915
War Diary	Renescure	07/06/1915	07/06/1915
War Diary	Hazebrouck	07/06/1915	08/06/1915

War Diary	Renescure	09/06/1915	09/06/1915
War Diary	Boesinghem	10/06/1915	10/06/1915
War Diary	Campayne	10/06/1915	10/06/1915
War Diary	Renescure	10/06/1915	10/06/1915
War Diary	Boesinghem	11/06/1915	11/06/1915
War Diary	Renescure	11/06/1915	12/06/1915
War Diary	Compayne	12/06/1915	12/06/1915
War Diary	Hazebrouck	12/06/1915	12/06/1915
War Diary	Steenbecque	13/06/1915	13/06/1915
War Diary	Renescure	13/06/1915	13/06/1915
War Diary	Wittes	14/06/1915	14/06/1915
War Diary	Steenbecque	14/06/1915	14/06/1915
War Diary	Hazebrouck	14/06/1915	14/06/1915
War Diary	Renescure	15/06/1915	15/06/1915
War Diary	Steenbecque	15/06/1915	15/06/1915
War Diary	Hazebrouck	15/06/1915	15/06/1915
War Diary	Renescure	16/06/1915	16/06/1915
War Diary	Steenbecque	16/06/1915	16/06/1915
War Diary	Hazebrouck	16/06/1915	16/06/1915
War Diary	Steenbecque	17/06/1915	17/06/1915
War Diary	Hazebrouck	18/06/1915	20/06/1915
War Diary	Blaringhem	21/06/1915	21/06/1915
War Diary	Steenbecque	21/06/1915	21/06/1915
War Diary	Wardrecque	21/06/1915	22/06/1915
War Diary	Hazebrouck	22/06/1915	22/06/1915
War Diary	Wardrecque	23/06/1915	23/06/1915
War Diary	Renescure	23/06/1915	23/06/1915
War Diary	Wardrecque	24/06/1915	24/06/1915
War Diary	Renescure	25/06/1915	25/06/1915
War Diary	Hazebrouck	25/06/1915	25/06/1915
War Diary	Wardrecque	26/06/1915	26/06/1915
War Diary	Renescure	27/06/1915	28/06/1915
War Diary	Hazebrouck	29/06/1915	29/06/1915
War Diary	Renescure	29/06/1915	30/06/1915
War Diary	Hazebrouck	30/06/1915	30/06/1915
Heading	12th Sanitary Section Vol VII		
War Diary	Renescure	01/07/1915	01/07/1915
War Diary	Hazebrouck	01/07/1915	01/07/1915
War Diary	Renescure	02/07/1915	02/07/1915
War Diary	Hazebrouck	02/07/1915	02/07/1915
War Diary	Wardrecques	03/07/1915	03/07/1915
War Diary	Hazebrouck	03/07/1915	03/07/1915
War Diary	Renescure	04/07/1915	04/07/1915
War Diary	Belseghem	05/07/1915	05/07/1915
War Diary	Renescure	05/07/1915	05/07/1915
War Diary	Hazebrouck	05/07/1915	05/07/1915
War Diary	Renescure	06/07/1915	06/07/1915
War Diary	Wardrecques	06/07/1915	06/07/1915
War Diary	Renescure	07/07/1915	07/07/1915
War Diary	Hazebrouck	07/07/1915	07/07/1915
War Diary	Renescure	08/07/1915	08/07/1915
War Diary	Hazebrouck	08/07/1915	08/07/1915
War Diary	Renescure	09/07/1915	09/07/1915
War Diary	Hazebrouck	09/07/1915	09/07/1915
War Diary	Renescure	10/07/1915	13/07/1915
War Diary	Sailly sur la Lis	13/07/1915	14/07/1915

War Diary	Heuringhem	15/07/1915	15/07/1915
War Diary	Sailly	15/07/1915	15/07/1915
War Diary	Heuringhem	16/07/1915	16/07/1915
War Diary	Pihem	16/07/1915	16/07/1915
War Diary	Grand Bois	16/07/1915	16/07/1915
War Diary	Heuringhem	16/07/1915	16/07/1915
War Diary	Sailly	16/07/1915	16/07/1915
War Diary	Sercus	17/07/1915	17/07/1915
War Diary	Heuringhem	17/07/1915	17/07/1915
War Diary	Pihem	17/07/1915	17/07/1915
War Diary	Heuringhem	17/07/1915	17/07/1915
War Diary	Sailly	17/07/1915	17/07/1915
War Diary	Sercus	18/07/1915	18/07/1915
War Diary	Pihem	18/07/1915	18/07/1915
War Diary	Heuringhem	19/07/1915	20/07/1915
War Diary	Sercus	19/07/1915	20/07/1915
War Diary	Heuringhem	20/07/1915	21/07/1915
War Diary	Quiestede	21/07/1915	21/07/1915
War Diary	Sercus	21/07/1915	21/07/1915
War Diary	Heuringhem	22/07/1915	22/07/1915
War Diary	Sercus	22/07/1915	22/07/1915
War Diary	Heuringhem	23/07/1915	23/07/1915
War Diary	Sercus	23/07/1915	23/07/1915
War Diary	Elverdinghe Belgium	23/07/1915	23/07/1915
War Diary	Sercus	24/07/1915	24/07/1915
War Diary	Morbecque	24/07/1915	24/07/1915
War Diary	Heuringhem	24/07/1915	24/07/1915
War Diary	Grand Bois	24/07/1915	24/07/1915
War Diary	Sercus	24/07/1915	24/07/1915
War Diary	Elverdinghe	24/07/1915	25/07/1915
War Diary	Sercus	25/07/1915	26/07/1915
War Diary	Heuringhem	26/07/1915	26/07/1915
War Diary	Elverdinghe	26/07/1915	26/07/1915
War Diary	Sercus	27/07/1915	27/07/1915
War Diary	Elverdinghe	27/07/1915	28/07/1915
War Diary	Heuringhem	28/07/1915	28/07/1915
War Diary	Elverdinghe	29/07/1915	29/07/1915
War Diary	Heuringhem	29/07/1915	29/07/1915
War Diary	Baeseghem	30/07/1915	30/07/1915
War Diary	Elverdinghe	30/07/1915	30/07/1915
War Diary	Heuringhem	30/07/1915	30/07/1915
War Diary	Baeseyhem	31/07/1915	31/07/1915
War Diary	Elverdinghe	31/07/1915	31/07/1915
War Diary	Heuringhem	31/07/1915	31/07/1915
Heading	12th Sany: Section Vol VIII From 1st To 31st Aug. 1915		
War Diary	Heuringhem	01/08/1915	01/08/1915
War Diary	Elverdinghe	01/08/1915	01/08/1915
War Diary	Boeseghem	01/08/1915	01/08/1915
War Diary	Heuringhem	02/08/1915	02/08/1915
War Diary	Elverdinghe	02/08/1915	02/08/1915
War Diary	Boeseghem	02/08/1915	02/08/1915
War Diary	Heuringhem	03/08/1915	03/08/1915
War Diary	Elverdinghe	03/08/1915	03/08/1915
War Diary	Boeseghem	03/08/1915	03/08/1915
War Diary	Heuringhem	04/08/1915	05/08/1915

War Diary	Elverdinghe	04/08/1915	04/08/1915
War Diary	Therouanne	04/08/1915	04/08/1915
War Diary	Heuringhem	05/08/1915	05/08/1915
War Diary	Elverdinghe	05/08/1915	05/08/1915
War Diary	Therouanne	05/08/1915	05/08/1915
War Diary	Heuringhem To Radinghem	06/08/1915	06/08/1915
War Diary	Radinghem	07/08/1915	08/08/1915
War Diary	Wandonne	07/08/1915	07/08/1915
War Diary	Linghem	07/08/1915	07/08/1915
War Diary	Radinghem	08/08/1915	08/08/1915
War Diary	Wandonne	08/08/1915	08/08/1915
War Diary	Linghem	08/08/1915	08/08/1915
War Diary	Radinghem	09/08/1915	09/08/1915
War Diary	Arques	09/08/1915	09/08/1915
War Diary	Fauquembergues	09/08/1915	09/08/1915
War Diary	Linghem	09/08/1915	09/08/1915
War Diary	Radinghem	10/08/1915	10/08/1915
War Diary	Fauquembergues	10/08/1915	10/08/1915
War Diary	Dennebroeucq	10/08/1915	10/08/1915
War Diary	Flechinelle Colliery	10/08/1915	10/08/1915
War Diary	Hervarre	10/08/1915	10/08/1915
War Diary	Radinghem	11/08/1915	11/08/1915
War Diary	Dennebroeucq	11/08/1915	11/08/1915
War Diary	Linghem	11/08/1915	11/08/1915
War Diary	Fauquembergues	11/08/1915	11/08/1915
War Diary	Radinghem	12/08/1915	12/08/1915
War Diary	Linghem	12/08/1915	12/08/1915
War Diary	Fauquembergues	12/08/1915	12/08/1915
War Diary	Radinghem	13/08/1915	13/08/1915
War Diary	Fauquembergues	13/08/1915	13/08/1915
War Diary	Linghem	13/08/1915	13/08/1915
War Diary	Radinghem	14/08/1915	14/08/1915
War Diary	Linghem	14/08/1915	14/08/1915
War Diary	Fauquembergues	14/08/1915	14/08/1915
War Diary	Radinghem	15/08/1915	15/08/1915
War Diary	Fauquembergues	15/08/1915	15/08/1915
War Diary	Linghem	15/08/1915	15/08/1915
War Diary	Radinghem	16/08/1915	16/08/1915
War Diary	Fauquembergues	16/08/1915	16/08/1915
War Diary	Linghem	16/08/1915	16/08/1915
War Diary	Radinghem	17/08/1915	17/08/1915
War Diary	Fauquembergues	17/08/1915	17/08/1915
War Diary	Linghem	17/08/1915	17/08/1915
War Diary	Radinghem	18/08/1915	18/08/1915
War Diary	Fauquembergues	18/08/1915	18/08/1915
War Diary	Linghem	18/08/1915	18/08/1915
War Diary	Radinghem	19/08/1915	19/08/1915
War Diary	Fauquembergues	19/08/1915	19/08/1915
War Diary	Wandonne	19/08/1915	19/08/1915
War Diary	Coyecque	19/08/1915	19/08/1915
War Diary	Radinghem	20/08/1915	20/08/1915
War Diary	Fauquembergues	20/08/1915	20/08/1915
War Diary	Radinghem	21/08/1915	21/08/1915
War Diary	Estree Blanche	21/08/1915	21/08/1915
War Diary	Fruges	21/08/1915	21/08/1915
War Diary	Fauquembergues	21/08/1915	21/08/1915

War Diary	Radinghem	22/08/1915	22/08/1915
War Diary	Estree Blanche	22/08/1915	22/08/1915
War Diary	Fruges	22/08/1915	22/08/1915
War Diary	Fauquembergues	22/08/1915	22/08/1915
War Diary	Radinghem	23/08/1915	23/08/1915
War Diary	Estree Blanche	23/08/1915	23/08/1915
War Diary	Fruges	23/08/1915	23/08/1915
War Diary	Fauquembergues	23/08/1915	23/08/1915
War Diary	Radinghem	24/08/1915	24/08/1915
War Diary	Estree Blanche	24/08/1915	24/08/1915
War Diary	Fruges	24/08/1915	24/08/1915
War Diary	Fauquembergues	24/08/1915	24/08/1915
War Diary	Radinghem	25/08/1915	25/08/1915
War Diary	Fruges	25/08/1915	25/08/1915
War Diary	Estree Blanche	25/08/1915	25/08/1915
War Diary	Coyecque	25/08/1915	25/08/1915
War Diary	Wandonne	25/08/1915	25/08/1915
War Diary	Fauquembergues	25/08/1915	25/08/1915
War Diary	Radinghem	26/08/1915	26/08/1915
War Diary	Fruges	26/08/1915	26/08/1915
War Diary	Nedon	26/08/1915	26/08/1915
War Diary	Hazebrouck	26/08/1915	26/08/1915
War Diary	Fauquembergues	26/08/1915	26/08/1915
War Diary	Radinghem	27/08/1915	27/08/1915
War Diary	Fruges	27/08/1915	27/08/1915
War Diary	Nedon	27/08/1915	27/08/1915
War Diary	Fauquembergues	27/08/1915	27/08/1915
War Diary	Radinghem	28/08/1915	28/08/1915
War Diary	Fruges	28/08/1915	28/08/1915
War Diary	Nedon	28/08/1915	28/08/1915
War Diary	Fauquembergues	28/08/1915	28/08/1915
War Diary	Radinghem	29/08/1915	29/08/1915
War Diary	Fruges	29/08/1915	29/08/1915
War Diary	Fauquembrgues	29/08/1915	29/08/1915
War Diary	Nedon	29/08/1915	29/08/1915
War Diary	Radinghem	30/08/1915	30/08/1915
War Diary	Fruges	30/08/1915	30/08/1915
War Diary	Nedon	30/08/1915	30/08/1915
War Diary	Fauquembergues	30/08/1915	30/08/1915
War Diary	Redinghem	31/08/1915	31/08/1915
War Diary	Nedon	31/08/1915	31/08/1915
War Diary	Fauquembrgs	31/08/1915	31/08/1915
Miscellaneous	Appendix No. 3 Out of Bound Notice Contagious Disease Prohibited To Troops		
Heading	3rd Cavalry Division 12th Sanitary Section Vol IX Sept 15		
War Diary	Redinghem	01/09/1915	01/09/1915
War Diary	Nedon	01/09/1915	01/09/1915
War Diary	Fauquembergues	01/09/1915	01/09/1915
War Diary	Fruges	01/09/1915	01/09/1915
War Diary	Radinghem	02/09/1915	02/09/1915
War Diary	Nedon	02/09/1915	02/09/1915
War Diary	Fauquembergues	02/09/1915	02/09/1915
War Diary	Fruges	02/09/1915	02/09/1915
War Diary	Radinghem	03/09/1915	03/09/1915
War Diary	Nedon	03/09/1915	03/09/1915

War Diary	Fauquembergues	03/09/1915	03/09/1915
War Diary	Fruges	03/09/1915	03/09/1915
War Diary	Radinghem	04/09/1915	04/09/1915
War Diary	Waudonne	04/09/1915	04/09/1915
War Diary	Nedon	04/09/1915	04/09/1915
War Diary	Fauquembergues	04/09/1915	04/09/1915
War Diary	Fruges	04/09/1915	04/09/1915
War Diary	Radinghem	05/09/1915	05/09/1915
War Diary	Nedon	05/09/1915	05/09/1915
War Diary	Fauquembergues	05/09/1915	05/09/1915
War Diary	Fruges	05/09/1915	05/09/1915
War Diary	Radinghem	01/09/1915	01/09/1915
War Diary	Nedon	01/09/1915	01/09/1915
War Diary	Fauquembergues	01/09/1915	01/09/1915
War Diary	Fruges	01/09/1915	01/09/1915
War Diary	Radinghem	02/09/1915	02/09/1915
War Diary	Nedon	02/09/1915	02/09/1915
War Diary	Fauquembergues	02/09/1915	02/09/1915
War Diary	Fruges	02/09/1915	02/09/1915
War Diary	Radinghem	03/09/1915	03/09/1915
War Diary	Nedon	03/09/1915	03/09/1915
War Diary	Fauquembergues	03/09/1915	03/09/1915
War Diary	Fruges	03/09/1915	03/09/1915
War Diary	Radinghem	04/09/1915	04/09/1915
War Diary	Wandonne	04/09/1915	04/09/1915
War Diary	Nedon	04/09/1915	04/09/1915
War Diary	Fauquembergues	04/09/1915	04/09/1915
War Diary	Fruges	04/09/1915	04/09/1915
War Diary	Radinghem	05/09/1915	05/09/1915
War Diary	Nedon	05/09/1915	05/09/1915
War Diary	Fauquembergues	05/09/1915	05/09/1915
War Diary	Fruges	05/09/1915	05/09/1915
War Diary	Radinghem	06/09/1915	06/09/1915
War Diary	Nedon	06/09/1915	06/09/1915
War Diary	Fauquembergues	06/09/1915	06/09/1915
War Diary	Fruges	06/09/1915	06/09/1915
War Diary	Radinghem	07/09/1915	07/09/1915
War Diary	Nedon	07/09/1915	07/09/1915
War Diary	Fruges	07/09/1915	07/09/1915
War Diary	Radinghem	08/09/1915	08/09/1915
War Diary	Fauquembergues	07/09/1915	07/09/1915
War Diary	Radinghem	08/09/1915	08/09/1915
War Diary	Caupelle Veille	08/09/1915	08/09/1915
War Diary	Fauquembergues	08/09/1915	08/09/1915
War Diary	Radinghem	09/09/1915	09/09/1915
War Diary	Caupelle Veille	09/09/1915	09/09/1915
War Diary	Febvin Palfart	09/09/1915	09/09/1915
War Diary	Fauquembergues Fruges	09/09/1915	09/09/1915
War Diary	Radinghem	10/09/1915	10/09/1915
War Diary	Febvin Palfart	10/09/1915	10/09/1915
War Diary	Fauquembergues Fruges	10/09/1915	10/09/1915
War Diary	Radinghem	11/09/1915	11/09/1915
War Diary	Felvin Palpart	11/09/1915	11/09/1915
War Diary	Fauquembergues Fruges	11/09/1915	11/09/1915
War Diary	Radinghem	12/09/1915	12/09/1915
War Diary	Felvin Palpart	12/09/1915	12/09/1915

War Diary	Fruges	12/09/1915	12/09/1915
War Diary	Radinghem	13/09/1915	13/09/1915
War Diary	Felvin Palpart	13/09/1915	13/09/1915
War Diary	Fauquembergues	13/09/1915	13/09/1915
War Diary	Radinghem	14/09/1915	14/09/1915
War Diary	Fleehin	14/09/1915	14/09/1915
War Diary	Fruges	14/09/1915	14/09/1915
War Diary	Fauquembergues	14/09/1915	14/09/1915
War Diary	Radinghem	15/09/1915	15/09/1915
War Diary	Fleehin	15/09/1915	15/09/1915
War Diary	Fruges	15/09/1915	15/09/1915
War Diary	Fauquembergues	15/09/1915	15/09/1915
War Diary	Radinghem	16/09/1915	16/09/1915
War Diary	Wandonne	16/09/1915	16/09/1915
War Diary	Fruges	16/09/1915	16/09/1915
War Diary	Fauquembergues	16/09/1915	16/09/1915
War Diary	Radinghem	17/09/1915	17/09/1915
War Diary	Fauquembergues	17/09/1915	17/09/1915
War Diary	Fruges	17/09/1915	17/09/1915
War Diary	Radinghem	18/09/1915	18/09/1915
War Diary	Fleehin	18/09/1915	18/09/1915
War Diary	Fruges	18/09/1915	18/09/1915
War Diary	Fauquembergues	18/09/1915	18/09/1915
War Diary	Radinghem	19/09/1915	19/09/1915
War Diary	Wandonne	19/09/1915	19/09/1915
War Diary	Fruges	19/09/1915	19/09/1915
War Diary	Fauquembergues	19/09/1915	19/09/1915
War Diary	Radinghem	20/09/1915	20/09/1915
War Diary	Fleehin	20/09/1915	20/09/1915
War Diary	Fruges	20/09/1915	20/09/1915
War Diary	Fauquembergues	20/09/1915	20/09/1915
War Diary	Radinghem	21/09/1915	21/09/1915
War Diary	Westrehem (near Dhemanne)	22/09/1915	22/09/1915
War Diary	Westrehem	23/09/1915	23/09/1915
War Diary	Westrehem	24/09/1915	24/09/1915
War Diary	Lalruisierre	25/09/1915	26/09/1915
War Diary	Rincq	27/09/1915	30/09/1915
Heading	3rd Cavalry Division Summarised but not Copied 12th Sanitary Section Vol X Oct 15		
War Diary	Rincq	01/10/1915	07/10/1915
War Diary	Ferfay	08/10/1915	08/10/1915
War Diary	Cauchy a la Tour	08/10/1915	08/10/1915
War Diary	Auchelle	08/10/1915	08/10/1915
War Diary	Rincq	09/10/1915	09/10/1915
War Diary	Ferfay	09/10/1915	09/10/1915
War Diary	Rincq	10/10/1915	10/10/1915
War Diary	Reinbert	10/10/1915	10/10/1915
War Diary	Rincq	11/10/1915	11/10/1915
War Diary	Hurionville	11/10/1915	11/10/1915
War Diary	Rincq	12/10/1915	12/10/1915
War Diary	Burbure	12/10/1915	12/10/1915
War Diary	Rincq	13/10/1915	13/10/1915
War Diary	Lillers	13/10/1915	13/10/1915
War Diary	Rincq	14/10/1915	14/10/1915
War Diary	Lieres	14/10/1915	14/10/1915
War Diary	Bourecq	14/10/1915	14/10/1915

War Diary	Rincq	15/10/1915	15/10/1915
War Diary	Ecquedecques	15/10/1915	15/10/1915
War Diary	Rincq	16/10/1915	16/10/1915
War Diary	Reinbert	16/10/1915	16/10/1915
War Diary	Rincq	17/10/1915	17/10/1915
War Diary	Hurionville	17/10/1915	17/10/1915
War Diary	Ferfay	17/10/1915	17/10/1915
War Diary	Rincq	18/10/1915	18/10/1915
War Diary	Auchelle	18/10/1915	18/10/1915
War Diary	Reinbert	18/10/1915	18/10/1915
War Diary	Burbure	18/10/1915	18/10/1915
War Diary	Rincq	19/10/1915	19/10/1915
War Diary	Fruges	19/10/1915	19/10/1915
War Diary	Fruges	20/10/1915	23/10/1915
War Diary	Laires	23/10/1915	23/10/1915
War Diary	Fruges	24/10/1915	25/10/1915
War Diary	Capelle Sur La Lys	25/10/1915	25/10/1915
War Diary	Flechinelle	25/10/1915	25/10/1915
War Diary	Fruges	26/10/1915	26/10/1915
War Diary	Capelle Sur La Lys	26/10/1915	26/10/1915
War Diary	Fruges	27/10/1915	27/10/1915
War Diary	Vincly	27/10/1915	27/10/1915
War Diary	Mattringhem	28/10/1915	28/10/1915
War Diary	Enquin Les Mines	28/10/1915	28/10/1915
War Diary	Hezecques	28/10/1915	28/10/1915
War Diary	Ligny Les Aires	28/10/1915	28/10/1915
War Diary	Fruges	29/10/1915	29/10/1915
War Diary	Mattringhem	29/10/1915	29/10/1915
War Diary	Beaumetz Les Aire	30/10/1915	30/10/1915
War Diary	Flechin	30/10/1915	30/10/1915
War Diary	Mattringhem	31/10/1915	31/10/1915
Heading	No. 12 Sanitary Section 3rd Cav Div Nov Vol XI Summarised but not Copied		
War Diary	Mattringhem	01/11/1915	01/11/1915
War Diary	Fruges	02/11/1915	02/11/1915
War Diary	Rumilly	02/11/1915	02/11/1915
War Diary	Fruges	03/11/1915	03/11/1915
War Diary	Fontaines Les Hermans	03/11/1915	03/11/1915
War Diary	Arenttes	03/11/1915	03/11/1915
War Diary	Fruges	04/11/1915	04/11/1915
War Diary	Dennebroeucq	04/11/1915	04/11/1915
War Diary	Mattringhem	04/11/1915	04/11/1915
War Diary	Fruges	05/11/1915	05/11/1915
War Diary	Ligny Les Aire	05/11/1915	05/11/1915
War Diary	Fruges	06/11/1915	09/11/1915
War Diary	Quderdom	09/11/1915	09/11/1915
War Diary	Fruges	10/11/1915	10/11/1915
War Diary	Flechinelle	11/11/1915	11/11/1915
War Diary	Fruges	11/11/1915	12/11/1915
War Diary	Flechinelle	12/11/1915	13/11/1915
War Diary	Fruges	13/11/1915	15/11/1915
War Diary	St Omer	15/11/1915	15/11/1915
War Diary	Fruges	16/11/1915	20/11/1915
War Diary	Crecquy	20/11/1915	20/11/1915
War Diary	Fruges	21/11/1915	21/11/1915
War Diary	Hesmondes	21/11/1915	21/11/1915

War Diary	Fruges	22/11/1915	23/11/1915
War Diary	Huequecliers	23/11/1915	24/11/1915
War Diary	Rimboval Embry Hesmondes	24/11/1915	24/11/1915
War Diary	Fruges	25/11/1915	25/11/1915
War Diary	Huequecliers	25/11/1915	25/11/1915
War Diary	Fruges	26/11/1915	27/11/1915
War Diary	Offin	27/11/1915	28/11/1915
War Diary	Fruges	28/11/1915	29/11/1915
War Diary	Offin	29/11/1915	29/11/1915
War Diary	Fruges	30/11/1915	30/11/1915
War Diary	Offin	30/11/1915	30/11/1915
Heading	3rd Cav Div. 12th Sanitary Sec Dec Val XII		
Miscellaneous	G.H. Qrs., 3rd Echelon.	31/01/1916	31/01/1916
Miscellaneous	O/c R.A.M.C. Seen.	30/01/1916	30/01/1916
War Diary	Fruges	01/12/1915	01/12/1915
War Diary	Offin	01/12/1915	01/12/1915
War Diary	Nandville	01/12/1915	01/12/1915
War Diary	Fruges	02/12/1915	02/12/1915
War Diary	Offin	02/12/1915	02/12/1915
War Diary	Fruges	03/12/1915	03/12/1915
War Diary	Offin	03/12/1915	03/12/1915
War Diary	Fruges	04/12/1915	04/12/1915
War Diary	Offin	04/12/1915	04/12/1915
War Diary	Bellevue	04/12/1915	04/12/1915
War Diary	Fruges	05/12/1915	07/12/1915
War Diary	Rumilly	07/12/1915	07/12/1915
War Diary	Crequy	07/12/1915	07/12/1915
War Diary	Fruges	08/12/1915	08/12/1915
War Diary	Crequy	08/12/1915	08/12/1915
War Diary	Fruges	09/12/1915	09/12/1915
War Diary	Crequy	09/12/1915	09/12/1915
War Diary	Rumilly	09/12/1915	09/12/1915
War Diary	Humbert	09/12/1915	09/12/1915
War Diary	Fruges	10/12/1915	10/12/1915
War Diary	Henly Niequinghem	10/12/1915	10/12/1915
War Diary	Fruges	11/12/1915	11/12/1915
War Diary	Crequy	11/12/1915	11/12/1915
War Diary	Fruges	12/12/1915	12/12/1915
War Diary	Crequy	12/12/1915	12/12/1915
War Diary	Caupille Villie	12/12/1915	12/12/1915
War Diary	Fruges	13/12/1915	13/12/1915
War Diary	Crequy	13/12/1915	13/12/1915
War Diary	Duilen	13/12/1915	13/12/1915
War Diary	Fruges	14/12/1915	14/12/1915
War Diary	Crequy	14/12/1915	14/12/1915
War Diary	Fruges	15/12/1915	15/12/1915
War Diary	Torcy	15/12/1915	15/12/1915
War Diary	Offin	15/12/1915	15/12/1915
War Diary	Fruges	16/12/1915	16/12/1915
War Diary	Torcy	16/12/1915	16/12/1915
War Diary	Marenla	16/12/1915	16/12/1915
War Diary	Fruges	17/12/1915	17/12/1915
War Diary	Royon	17/12/1915	17/12/1915
War Diary	Fruges	18/12/1915	18/12/1915
War Diary	Coupille Heune	18/12/1915	18/12/1915
War Diary	Fruges	19/12/1915	19/12/1915

War Diary	Hesmond	19/12/1915	19/12/1915
War Diary	Fruges	20/12/1915	20/12/1915
War Diary	Hesmond	20/12/1915	20/12/1915
War Diary	Fruges	21/12/1915	21/12/1915
War Diary	Hesmond	21/12/1915	21/12/1915
War Diary	Embry	21/12/1915	21/12/1915
War Diary	Fruges	22/12/1915	22/12/1915
War Diary	Ledeghem	22/12/1915	22/12/1915
War Diary	Mamant	22/12/1915	22/12/1915
War Diary	Offin	22/12/1915	22/12/1915
War Diary	Fruges	23/12/1915	24/12/1915
War Diary	Mamant	24/12/1915	24/12/1915
War Diary	Fruges	25/12/1915	28/12/1915
War Diary	Sempy	28/12/1915	28/12/1915
War Diary	Fruges	29/12/1915	29/12/1915
War Diary	Libieca Hesmond	29/12/1915	29/12/1915
War Diary	Fruges	30/12/1915	30/12/1915
War Diary	St Denoeux	30/12/1915	30/12/1915
War Diary	Offin	30/12/1915	30/12/1915
War Diary	Fruges	31/12/1915	31/12/1915
War Diary	St Denoeux	31/12/1915	31/12/1915
Heading	3rd Cav. Div. Sanitary Sect (No/12 Sary Section Jan. 1916 Vol I		
Miscellaneous	Christmas Messages From His Majesty The King.		
Miscellaneous	Special Order of the Day.	18/12/1916	18/12/1916
War Diary	Fruges	27/01/1916	27/01/1916
War Diary	Sailly Lab	27/01/1916	27/01/1916
War Diary	Noyelle	27/01/1916	27/01/1916
War Diary	Fruges	28/01/1916	28/01/1916
War Diary	Sailly	28/01/1916	28/01/1916
War Diary	Noyelles	28/01/1916	29/01/1916
War Diary	Sailly	30/01/1916	31/01/1916
War Diary	Fruges	23/01/1916	23/01/1916
War Diary	Sailly Labourse	23/01/1916	23/01/1916
War Diary	Fruges	24/01/1916	24/01/1916
War Diary	Sailly	24/01/1916	24/01/1916
War Diary	Noyelles	24/01/1916	24/01/1916
War Diary	Sailly	25/01/1916	25/01/1916
War Diary	Fruges	25/01/1916	26/01/1916
War Diary	Sailly Labourse	26/01/1916	26/01/1916
War Diary	Noyelles	26/01/1916	26/01/1916
War Diary	Sailly Labourse	26/01/1915	26/01/1915
War Diary	Noyelles	26/01/1916	26/01/1916
War Diary	Sailly	16/01/1916	16/01/1916
War Diary	Labourse	16/01/1916	16/01/1916
War Diary	Noyelles	17/01/1916	17/01/1916
War Diary	Fruges	18/01/1916	18/01/1916
War Diary	Sailly	18/01/1916	18/01/1916
War Diary	Labourse	18/01/1916	18/01/1916
War Diary	Noyelles	18/01/1916	18/01/1916
War Diary	Fruges	19/01/1916	19/01/1916
War Diary	Noyelles	19/01/1916	19/01/1916
War Diary	Sally Labourse	19/01/1916	20/01/1916
War Diary	Noyelles	20/01/1916	21/01/1916
War Diary	Sailly Lab	22/01/1916	22/01/1916
War Diary	Noyelles	22/01/1916	22/01/1916

War Diary	Noyelles	10/01/1916	10/01/1916
War Diary	Verquingneul	10/01/1916	11/01/1916
War Diary	Noyelles	11/01/1916	11/01/1916
War Diary	Fruges	11/01/1916	12/01/1916
War Diary	Noyelles	12/01/1916	15/01/1916
War Diary	Fruges	01/01/1916	02/01/1916
War Diary	Maverla	02/01/1916	02/01/1916
War Diary	St Denoeux	03/01/1916	03/01/1916
War Diary	Aux-En-Issant	03/01/1916	03/01/1916
War Diary	Fruges	03/01/1916	03/01/1916
War Diary	Covelle Mene	03/01/1916	03/01/1916
War Diary	Fruges	04/01/1916	04/01/1916
War Diary	Hesmond	05/01/1916	05/01/1916
War Diary	Fruges	06/01/1916	06/01/1916
War Diary	Verquingneul	06/01/1916	07/01/1916
War Diary	Fruges	07/01/1916	07/01/1916
War Diary	Verquingneul	08/01/1916	08/01/1916
War Diary	Noyelles	08/01/1916	09/01/1916
War Diary	Fruges	09/01/1916	09/01/1916
Heading	3rd Cav. Div. 12th Sary Section Feb 1916		
Heading	Sanitary Section 3 Cav Div Feb Vol XIII		
War Diary	Fruges	01/02/1916	01/02/1916
War Diary	Noyelles	01/02/1916	01/02/1916
War Diary	Fruges	02/02/1916	02/02/1916
War Diary	Noyelles	02/02/1916	02/02/1916
War Diary	Fruges	03/02/1916	03/02/1916
War Diary	Noyelles	03/02/1916	03/02/1916
War Diary	Fruges	04/02/1916	04/02/1916
War Diary	Noyelles	04/02/1916	04/02/1916
War Diary	Sailly	04/02/1916	04/02/1916
War Diary	Fruges	05/02/1916	05/02/1916
War Diary	Noyelles	05/02/1916	05/02/1916
War Diary	Sailly	05/02/1916	05/02/1916
War Diary	Fruges	06/02/1916	06/02/1916
War Diary	Sailly	06/02/1916	06/02/1916
War Diary	Noyelles	06/02/1916	06/02/1916
War Diary	Fruges	07/02/1916	07/02/1916
War Diary	Amequin	07/02/1916	07/02/1916
War Diary	Sailly	07/02/1916	07/02/1916
War Diary	Noyelles	07/02/1916	07/02/1916
War Diary	Fruges	08/02/1916	08/02/1916
War Diary	Labourse	08/02/1916	08/02/1916
War Diary	Noyelles	08/02/1916	08/02/1916
War Diary	Fruges	09/02/1916	09/02/1916
War Diary	Noyelles	09/02/1916	09/02/1916
War Diary	Fruges	10/02/1916	10/02/1916
War Diary	Noyelles	10/02/1916	10/02/1916
War Diary	Fruges	11/02/1916	11/02/1916
War Diary	Noyelles	11/02/1916	11/02/1916
War Diary	Sailly	11/02/1916	11/02/1916
War Diary	Fruges	12/02/1916	12/02/1916
War Diary	Noyelles	12/02/1916	12/02/1916
War Diary	Fruges	13/02/1916	13/02/1916
War Diary	Noyelles	13/02/1916	13/02/1916
War Diary	Fruges	14/02/1916	14/02/1916
War Diary	Aix en Issart	14/02/1916	14/02/1916

War Diary	Noyelles	14/02/1916	14/02/1916
War Diary	Fruges	15/02/1916	15/02/1916
War Diary	Hesmond	15/02/1916	15/02/1916
War Diary	Sailly	15/02/1916	15/02/1916
War Diary	Fruges	16/02/1916	17/02/1916
War Diary	Fruges Boubers	18/02/1916	18/02/1916
War Diary	Fruges	19/02/1916	20/02/1916
War Diary	Fruges Boubers	21/02/1916	21/02/1916
War Diary	Fruges	22/02/1916	22/02/1916
War Diary	Fruges Boubers	23/02/1916	24/02/1916
War Diary	Fruges	25/02/1916	29/02/1916
War Diary	Embry	29/02/1916	29/02/1916
Heading	No.12 Sanitary Section March 1916		
Heading	3 C 12 Sanitary Sec Vol XIV		
War Diary	Hesmond	01/03/1916	01/03/1916
War Diary	Fruges	01/03/1916	01/03/1916
War Diary	Herly	01/03/1916	01/03/1916
War Diary	Pollier	02/03/1916	02/03/1916
War Diary	Herly	02/03/1916	02/03/1916
War Diary	Hesmond	02/03/1916	02/03/1916
War Diary	Fruges	02/03/1916	02/03/1916
War Diary	Boubers Hesmond Anesnes	03/03/1916	03/03/1916
War Diary	Fruges	03/03/1916	03/03/1916
War Diary	Embry	03/03/1916	03/03/1916
War Diary	Herly	03/03/1916	03/03/1916
War Diary	Hesmond	04/03/1916	04/03/1916
War Diary	Herly	04/03/1916	04/03/1916
War Diary	Boubers	04/03/1916	04/03/1916
War Diary	Boubers	05/03/1916	05/03/1916
War Diary	St Denoeux	05/03/1916	05/03/1916
War Diary	Embry	05/03/1916	05/03/1916
War Diary	Hesmond	06/03/1916	06/03/1916
War Diary	Embry	06/03/1916	06/03/1916
War Diary	Fruges	06/03/1916	06/03/1916
War Diary	Hesmond	06/03/1916	06/03/1916
War Diary	Boubers	07/03/1916	07/03/1916
War Diary	Fruges	07/03/1916	07/03/1916
War Diary	Pollier	08/03/1916	08/03/1916
War Diary	Embry	08/03/1916	08/03/1916
War Diary	Boubers	08/03/1916	08/03/1916
War Diary	Fruges	08/03/1916	08/03/1916
War Diary	Hesmond	08/03/1916	08/03/1916
War Diary	Embry	08/03/1916	08/03/1916
War Diary	Embry	09/03/1916	09/03/1916
War Diary	Fruges	09/03/1916	09/03/1916
War Diary	Hesmond	09/03/1916	09/03/1916
War Diary	Boubers	10/03/1916	10/03/1916
War Diary	Pollier	10/03/1916	10/03/1916
War Diary	Embry	10/03/1916	10/03/1916
War Diary	St Denoeux	10/03/1916	10/03/1916
War Diary	Fruges	10/03/1916	10/03/1916
War Diary	Fruges	11/03/1916	11/03/1916
War Diary	Embry	11/03/1916	11/03/1916
War Diary	Sempy	11/03/1916	11/03/1916
War Diary	Fruges	12/03/1916	13/03/1916
War Diary	Heuqueliers	13/03/1916	13/03/1916

War Diary	Boubers	13/03/1916	13/03/1916
War Diary	Embry St Demnout	13/03/1916	13/03/1916
War Diary	Fruges	14/03/1916	14/03/1916
War Diary	St Denoeux	14/03/1916	14/03/1916
War Diary	Boubers	14/03/1916	14/03/1916
War Diary	Hucquelliers	14/03/1916	14/03/1916
War Diary	Fruges	15/03/1916	15/03/1916
War Diary	Pollier	15/03/1916	15/03/1916
War Diary	Assomal	15/03/1916	15/03/1916
War Diary	Boubers	15/03/1916	15/03/1916
War Diary	Herly	15/03/1916	15/03/1916
War Diary	Aulin	15/03/1916	15/03/1916
War Diary	Royon	15/03/1916	15/03/1916
War Diary	Fruges	16/03/1916	16/03/1916
War Diary	Coupelle Neuve	16/03/1916	16/03/1916
War Diary	Fruges	17/03/1916	17/03/1916
War Diary	Marant	17/03/1916	17/03/1916
War Diary	Embry	17/03/1916	17/03/1916
War Diary	Sains-Les-Frenins	17/03/1916	17/03/1916
War Diary	Fruges	18/03/1916	18/03/1916
War Diary	Embry	18/03/1916	18/03/1916
War Diary	Aix-en-Issart	18/03/1916	18/03/1916
War Diary	Fruges	19/03/1916	19/03/1916
War Diary	Boubers	19/03/1916	19/03/1916
War Diary	Rimboval	19/03/1916	19/03/1916
War Diary	Wicquinghem	19/03/1916	19/03/1916
War Diary	Assonval	19/03/1916	19/03/1916
War Diary	Fruges	20/03/1916	20/03/1916
War Diary	Mamant	20/03/1916	20/03/1916
War Diary	Wicquinghem	20/03/1916	20/03/1916
War Diary	Embry	20/03/1916	20/03/1916
War Diary	Aix-en-Issart	20/03/1916	20/03/1916
War Diary	Tramecourt	20/03/1916	20/03/1916
War Diary	Fruges	21/03/1916	21/03/1916
War Diary	Verchocq	21/03/1916	21/03/1916
War Diary	Boubers	21/03/1916	21/03/1916
War Diary	Fruges	21/03/1916	21/03/1916
War Diary	Embry	21/03/1916	21/03/1916
War Diary	Coupelle Ville	21/03/1916	21/03/1916
War Diary	Fruges	22/03/1916	22/03/1916
War Diary	Embry	22/03/1916	22/03/1916
War Diary	Rimboval	22/03/1916	22/03/1916
War Diary	Fruges	23/03/1916	23/03/1916
War Diary	Embry	23/03/1916	23/03/1916
War Diary	Rollea	23/03/1916	23/03/1916
War Diary	Verchocq	23/03/1916	23/03/1916
War Diary	Creqhey	23/03/1916	23/03/1916
War Diary	Fruges	24/03/1916	24/03/1916
War Diary	Rollez	24/03/1916	24/03/1916
War Diary	Crequy	24/03/1916	24/03/1916
War Diary	St Denoeux	24/03/1916	24/03/1916
War Diary	Fruges	25/03/1916	25/03/1916
War Diary	Verchocq	25/03/1916	25/03/1916
War Diary	St Denoeux	25/03/1916	25/03/1916
War Diary	Tramecourt	25/03/1916	25/03/1916
War Diary	Fruges	26/03/1916	26/03/1916

War Diary	Huequecliers	26/03/1916	26/03/1916
War Diary	Rollez	26/03/1916	26/03/1916
War Diary	Huequecliers	26/03/1916	26/03/1916
War Diary	Fruges	27/03/1916	27/03/1916
War Diary	Bourainville	27/03/1916	27/03/1916
War Diary	Montreuil	27/03/1916	27/03/1916
War Diary	Fruges	28/03/1916	28/03/1916
War Diary	Marant	28/03/1916	28/03/1916
War Diary	Fruges	29/03/1916	29/03/1916
War Diary	Tramecourt	29/03/1916	29/03/1916
War Diary	Fruges	30/03/1916	30/03/1916
War Diary	Creqhey	30/03/1916	30/03/1916
War Diary	Hesmond	30/03/1916	30/03/1916
War Diary	Fruges	31/03/1916	31/03/1916
War Diary	Royow	31/03/1916	31/03/1916
Heading	No.12 Sanitary Section April-May 1916		
War Diary	Fruges	01/04/1916	02/04/1916
War Diary	Verchocq Rumilly	02/04/1916	02/04/1916
War Diary	Fruges	03/04/1916	03/04/1916
War Diary	Wicquinghem	03/04/1916	03/04/1916
War Diary	Fruges	04/04/1916	06/04/1916
War Diary	Aix-en-Issart	06/04/1916	06/04/1916
War Diary	Fruges	07/04/1916	09/04/1916
War Diary	Herly Bellune	09/04/1916	09/04/1916
War Diary	Fruges	10/04/1916	10/04/1916
War Diary	Loison	10/04/1916	10/04/1916
War Diary	Fruges	11/04/1916	12/04/1916
War Diary	Herequiliers	12/04/1916	12/04/1916
War Diary	Rollea	12/04/1916	12/04/1916
War Diary	Fruges	13/04/1916	15/04/1916
War Diary	Fransecourt	15/04/1916	15/04/1916
War Diary	Fruges	15/04/1916	17/04/1916
War Diary	Embry	17/04/1916	17/04/1916
War Diary	Fruges	18/04/1916	18/04/1916
War Diary	Predve	18/04/1916	18/04/1916
War Diary	Fruges	19/04/1916	19/04/1916
War Diary	Predve	19/04/1916	19/04/1916
War Diary	Fruges	20/04/1916	21/04/1916
War Diary	Embry	21/04/1916	21/04/1916
War Diary	Morles	21/04/1916	21/04/1916
War Diary	Fruges	22/04/1916	22/04/1916
War Diary	Blaingel	22/04/1916	22/04/1916
War Diary	Fruges	23/04/1916	24/04/1916
War Diary	Bourainville	24/04/1916	24/04/1916
War Diary	Fruges	25/04/1916	25/04/1916
War Diary	Offin	25/04/1916	25/04/1916
War Diary	Fruges	26/04/1916	26/04/1916
War Diary	Offin	26/04/1916	26/04/1916
War Diary	Fruges	27/04/1916	27/04/1916
War Diary	Offin	27/04/1916	27/04/1916
War Diary	Beauvainville	27/04/1916	27/04/1916
War Diary	Fruges	28/04/1916	28/04/1916
War Diary	Hesdin	28/04/1916	28/04/1916
War Diary	Fressin	28/04/1916	28/04/1916
War Diary	Fruges	29/04/1916	29/04/1916
War Diary	Embry	29/04/1916	29/04/1916

War Diary	Fruges	30/04/1916	30/04/1916
War Diary	Tramecourt	30/04/1916	30/04/1916
War Diary	Fruges	01/05/1916	02/05/1916
War Diary	Assonval	02/05/1916	02/05/1916
War Diary	Fruges	03/05/1916	03/05/1916
War Diary	Coupelle Neuve	03/05/1916	03/05/1916
War Diary	Fruges	04/05/1916	08/05/1916
War Diary	Humbert	08/05/1916	08/05/1916
War Diary	Fruges	09/05/1916	09/05/1916
War Diary	Humbert	09/05/1916	09/05/1916
War Diary	Fressin	09/05/1916	09/05/1916
War Diary	Fruges	10/05/1916	10/05/1916
War Diary	Humbert	10/05/1916	10/05/1916
War Diary	Fruges	11/05/1916	11/05/1916
War Diary	Humbert	11/05/1916	11/05/1916
War Diary	Truismanquis	11/05/1916	11/05/1916
War Diary	Fruges	12/05/1916	15/05/1916
War Diary	Maison Ponthieu	15/05/1916	15/05/1916
War Diary	Fruges	15/05/1916	16/05/1916
War Diary	Framecourt	16/05/1916	16/05/1916
War Diary	Fruges	17/05/1916	17/05/1916
War Diary	St Riquier	17/05/1916	17/05/1916
War Diary	Fruges	18/05/1916	19/05/1916
War Diary	Argemieers	19/05/1916	19/05/1916
War Diary	Fruges	20/05/1916	20/05/1916
War Diary	Comchy	20/05/1916	20/05/1916
War Diary	Fruges	21/05/1916	22/05/1916
War Diary	Cavron St Martin	22/05/1916	22/05/1916
War Diary	Framecourt	22/05/1916	22/05/1916
War Diary	Fruges	22/05/1916	23/05/1916
War Diary	Framecourt	23/05/1916	23/05/1916
War Diary	Fruges	24/05/1916	25/05/1916
War Diary	Crequy	25/05/1916	25/05/1916
War Diary	Rumilly	25/05/1916	25/05/1916
War Diary	Furges	25/05/1916	25/05/1916
War Diary	Fruges	26/05/1916	26/05/1916
War Diary	Rimboval	26/05/1916	26/05/1916
War Diary	Embry	26/05/1916	26/05/1916
War Diary	Hesmonds	26/05/1916	26/05/1916
War Diary	Fruges	27/05/1916	27/05/1916
War Diary	Quilen	27/05/1916	27/05/1916
War Diary	Aix-en-Issart	27/05/1916	27/05/1916
War Diary	Fruges	28/05/1916	28/05/1916
War Diary	Boubers	28/05/1916	28/05/1916
War Diary	Fruges	29/05/1916	29/05/1916
War Diary	Contes	29/05/1916	29/05/1916
War Diary	Fruges	30/05/1916	30/05/1916
War Diary	Rimboval	30/05/1916	30/05/1916
War Diary	Fruges	31/05/1916	31/05/1916
War Diary	Hesmonds Lubien	31/05/1916	31/05/1916
Heading	12th Sanitary Section June		
Miscellaneous	Committee for The Medical History of The War	13/09/1916	13/09/1916
War Diary	Fruges	01/06/1916	01/06/1916
War Diary	Fruges	02/06/1916	03/06/1916
War Diary	Boubers	03/06/1916	03/06/1916
War Diary	Fruges	04/06/1916	09/06/1916

War Diary	Coupelle Ville	09/06/1916	09/06/1916
War Diary	Fruges	10/06/1916	10/06/1916
War Diary	Coupelle Ville	10/06/1916	10/06/1916
War Diary	Fruges	11/06/1916	11/06/1916
War Diary	Furges	11/06/1916	11/06/1916
War Diary	Fruges	12/06/1916	12/06/1916
War Diary	Sunday	12/06/1916	12/06/1916
War Diary	Fruges	13/06/1916	14/06/1916
War Diary	Embry	14/06/1916	15/06/1916
War Diary	Fruges	15/06/1916	16/06/1916
War Diary	Loison Beauvainville	16/06/1916	16/06/1916
War Diary	Fruges	17/06/1916	18/06/1916
War Diary	Aix-en-Envy	18/06/1916	18/06/1916
War Diary	Fruges	19/06/1916	25/06/1916
War Diary	Domart-en-Ponthieu	26/06/1916	26/06/1916
War Diary	La Neuville	27/06/1916	02/07/1916
War Diary	Bonnay	02/07/1916	02/07/1916
War Diary	La Neuville	03/07/1916	03/07/1916
War Diary	Bonnay	03/07/1916	03/07/1916
War Diary	La Neuville	04/07/1916	04/07/1916
War Diary	Hallencourt	05/07/1916	06/07/1916
War Diary	Airaines	06/07/1916	06/07/1916
War Diary	Hallencourt	07/07/1916	08/07/1916
War Diary	Daours	09/07/1916	16/07/1916
War Diary	Corbie	16/07/1916	16/07/1916
War Diary	Daours	17/07/1916	17/07/1916
War Diary	Pont Noyelles	17/07/1916	17/07/1916
War Diary	Daours	18/07/1916	19/07/1916
War Diary	Corbie	19/07/1916	19/07/1916
War Diary	Daours	20/07/1916	20/07/1916
War Diary	Bonnay	20/07/1916	20/07/1916
War Diary	Daours	21/07/1916	21/07/1916
War Diary	La Neuville	21/07/1916	21/07/1916
War Diary	Daours	22/07/1916	22/07/1916
War Diary	Corbie	22/07/1916	22/07/1916
War Diary	Daours	23/07/1916	23/07/1916
War Diary	Corbie	23/07/1916	23/07/1916
War Diary	Daours	24/07/1916	24/07/1916
War Diary	Bonnay	24/07/1916	24/07/1916
War Diary	Daours	25/07/1916	25/07/1916
War Diary	Bonnay	25/07/1916	25/07/1916
War Diary	Daours	26/07/1916	26/07/1916
War Diary	Corbie	26/07/1916	26/07/1916
War Diary	La Neuville	26/07/1916	26/07/1916
War Diary	Daours	27/07/1916	27/07/1916
War Diary	Corbie	27/07/1916	27/07/1916
War Diary	La Neuville	27/07/1916	27/07/1916
War Diary	Daours	28/07/1916	28/07/1916
War Diary	Corbie	28/07/1916	28/07/1916
War Diary	La Neuville	28/07/1916	28/07/1916
War Diary	Corbie	28/07/1916	28/07/1916
War Diary	Daours	29/07/1916	29/07/1916
War Diary	Corbie	29/07/1916	29/07/1916
War Diary	Daours	30/07/1916	30/07/1916
War Diary	Corbie	30/07/1916	30/07/1916
War Diary	Daours	31/07/1916	31/07/1916

Heading	Diary of No 12 Sanitary Section Vol 19 Month Of August 1916			
War Diary	Daours		01/08/1916	01/08/1916
War Diary	St Quesnoy		02/08/1916	02/08/1916
War Diary	Yvrencheux		03/08/1916	04/08/1916
War Diary	Ligescourt		05/08/1916	05/08/1916
War Diary	Fruges		06/08/1916	07/08/1916
War Diary	Offin		07/08/1916	07/08/1916
War Diary	Fressur Wambercourt Lebiez offin & Beauvainville		07/08/1916	07/08/1916
War Diary	Fruges		08/08/1916	08/08/1916
War Diary	Offin		08/08/1916	08/08/1916
War Diary	Fruges		09/08/1916	09/08/1916
War Diary	Offin		09/08/1916	09/08/1916
War Diary	Fruges		10/08/1916	11/08/1916
War Diary	Lebriez		11/08/1916	11/08/1916
War Diary	Fruges		11/08/1916	11/08/1916
War Diary	Letilz		11/08/1916	11/08/1916
War Diary	Fruges		12/08/1916	12/08/1916
War Diary	Royon		12/08/1916	12/08/1916
War Diary	Fruges & Framecourt		13/08/1916	13/08/1916
War Diary	Fruges		13/08/1916	13/08/1916
War Diary	Cavron St Martin		13/08/1916	13/08/1916
War Diary	Fruges		14/08/1916	14/08/1916
War Diary	Wambercourt		14/08/1916	14/08/1916
War Diary	Fruges		14/08/1916	15/08/1916
War Diary	Teneur		15/08/1916	15/08/1916
War Diary	Fruges		16/08/1916	16/08/1916
War Diary	Teneur & Erin		16/08/1916	16/08/1916
War Diary	Fruges		17/08/1916	17/08/1916
War Diary	Fressin		17/08/1916	17/08/1916
War Diary	Fruges		18/08/1916	18/08/1916
War Diary	Blangy		18/08/1916	18/08/1916
War Diary	Auelery-Les-Hesdins		18/08/1916	18/08/1916
War Diary	Fruges		19/08/1916	19/08/1916
War Diary	Blangy		19/08/1916	19/08/1916
War Diary	Tramecourt		19/08/1916	19/08/1916
War Diary	Fruges		20/08/1916	20/08/1916
War Diary	Blingel		20/08/1916	20/08/1916
War Diary	Fruges		21/08/1916	21/08/1916
War Diary	Auchy		21/08/1916	21/08/1916
War Diary	Embry		21/08/1916	21/08/1916
War Diary	Royon		21/08/1916	21/08/1916
War Diary	Fruges		22/08/1916	22/08/1916
War Diary	Auchy		22/08/1916	22/08/1916
War Diary	Bouthes		22/08/1916	22/08/1916
War Diary	Fruges		23/08/1916	23/08/1916
War Diary	Auchy		23/08/1916	23/08/1916
War Diary	Boubers		23/08/1916	23/08/1916
War Diary	Fruges		24/08/1916	24/08/1916
War Diary	Grigny		24/08/1916	24/08/1916
War Diary	Fruges		25/08/1916	25/08/1916
War Diary	Royon		25/08/1916	25/08/1916
War Diary	Fruges		26/08/1916	28/08/1916
War Diary	Campelle Vielle		28/08/1916	28/08/1916
War Diary	Fruges		29/08/1916	29/08/1916
War Diary	Forey		29/08/1916	29/08/1916

War Diary	Framecourt	29/08/1916	29/08/1916
War Diary	Fruges	30/08/1916	30/08/1916
Heading	3rd Cav. Div. 12th Sanitary Section Sept 1916		
Heading	Diary of No 12 Sanitary Section September 1916		
War Diary	Fruges	01/09/1916	07/09/1916
War Diary	Fruges Aixen Ergny	08/09/1916	08/09/1916
War Diary	Fruges Hesmond	09/09/1916	09/09/1916
War Diary	Fruges To Guishart	10/09/1916	11/09/1916
War Diary	Guishart to Belloy-Sur-Sonne	12/09/1916	12/09/1916
War Diary	Belloy	13/09/1916	13/09/1916
War Diary	Belloy-Sur-Somme to Daours	14/09/1916	14/09/1916
War Diary	Daours	15/09/1916	21/09/1916
War Diary	Daours le Quesnoy	22/09/1916	22/09/1916
War Diary	Le Quesnoy Foohen Le Grand	23/09/1916	23/09/1916
War Diary	Frohen Le Grand Guiqny	24/09/1916	24/09/1916
War Diary	Guigny	25/09/1916	30/09/1916
Heading	3rd Cav Division No 12 Sanitary Section Oct 1916		
Heading	War Diary of No 12 Sanitary Section October 1916 Vol 21		
War Diary	Guigny	01/10/1916	01/10/1916
War Diary	Guigny to Capelle	02/10/1916	02/10/1916
War Diary	Capille	03/10/1916	04/10/1916
War Diary	Loison	04/10/1916	04/10/1916
War Diary	Capille	05/10/1916	18/10/1916
War Diary	Beauvainville	18/10/1916	18/10/1916
War Diary	Capille to Bois-Jean	19/10/1916	19/10/1916
War Diary	Bois-Jean	20/10/1916	27/10/1916
War Diary	Bois-Jean Merhimont	28/10/1916	28/10/1916
War Diary	Bois Jean Cregny	30/10/1916	30/10/1916
War Diary	Bois-Jean	31/10/1916	31/10/1916
Heading	Original Copy Dec 1916		
War Diary	Bois-Jean St Josse	31/12/1916	31/12/1916
War Diary	Bois-Jean	27/12/1916	27/12/1916
War Diary	Remount Buire Le Sec Marenla	27/12/1916	27/12/1916
War Diary	Bois-Jean	28/12/1916	28/12/1916
War Diary	Berh	28/12/1916	28/12/1916
War Diary	St. Jose	28/12/1916	28/12/1916
War Diary	Bois-Jean	29/12/1916	29/12/1916
War Diary	Bois-Jean	30/12/1916	30/12/1916
War Diary	Bois-Jean	01/12/1916	02/12/1916
War Diary	St Josse	02/12/1916	02/12/1916
War Diary	Bois-Jean	03/12/1916	07/12/1916
War Diary	Berheplege	07/12/1916	07/12/1916
War Diary	Bois-Jean	08/12/1916	08/12/1916
War Diary	Muhimart Plege	08/12/1916	08/12/1916
War Diary	Bois-Jean	09/12/1916	11/12/1916
War Diary	Canon St Martin	11/12/1916	11/12/1916
War Diary	Bois-Jean	12/12/1916	12/12/1916
War Diary	Muhiment Plege	12/12/1916	12/12/1916
War Diary	Bois-Jean	13/12/1916	15/12/1916
War Diary	Muhiment Plege	15/12/1916	15/12/1916
War Diary	Bois-Jean	16/12/1916	17/12/1916
War Diary	Wailly	17/12/1916	17/12/1916
War Diary	Bois Jean	18/12/1916	21/12/1916
War Diary	Bois Jean Buirelosie	21/12/1916	21/12/1916
War Diary	Bois Jean	22/12/1916	22/12/1916

War Diary	Bois Jean Compigneulles Petit		23/12/1916	23/12/1916
War Diary	Bois Jean		24/12/1916	26/12/1916
War Diary	Roussent Le Nr		26/12/1916	26/12/1916
Heading	3rd Cav. Div. No 12 Sanitary Section Dec 1916			
Heading	12 Saint Sec Vol 22 War Diary For The Month Of November 1916			
War Diary	Bois Jean		01/11/1916	01/11/1916
War Diary	Bois Jean		02/11/1916	02/11/1916
War Diary	Aix-en-Issart		02/11/1916	02/11/1916
War Diary	Bois Jean		03/11/1916	03/11/1916
War Diary	Torcy		03/11/1916	03/11/1916
War Diary	Bois-Jean		04/11/1916	07/11/1916
War Diary	Merhimont Plege		07/11/1916	07/11/1916
War Diary	Bois-Jean		08/11/1916	30/11/1916
Heading	3rd Cav Div.War Diary of No 12 Sanitary Section 2nd London Sanitary Company R.A.M.C. T.F. For January 1917			
War Diary	Bois Jean St Josse		01/01/1917	01/01/1917
War Diary	St Josse		01/01/1917	01/01/1917
War Diary	Bois Jean		02/01/1917	02/01/1917
War Diary	Mulimont Plage		02/01/1917	02/01/1917
War Diary	Evegny		02/01/1917	02/01/1917
War Diary	Bois Jean		03/01/1917	03/01/1917
War Diary	Mulimont Plage		03/01/1917	03/01/1917
War Diary	Bois Jean		04/01/1917	04/01/1917
War Diary	Mulimont Plage		04/01/1917	04/01/1917
War Diary	Bois Jean		05/01/1917	05/01/1917
War Diary	Compiqneulles Les Grandes		05/01/1917	05/01/1917
War Diary	Irepied		06/01/1917	06/01/1917
War Diary	Roussent		06/01/1917	06/01/1917
War Diary	Berk		06/01/1917	06/01/1917
War Diary	Irepied		07/01/1917	09/01/1917
War Diary	Hesmond		09/01/1917	09/01/1917
War Diary	Irepied		10/01/1917	10/01/1917
War Diary	Evegny		10/01/1917	10/01/1917
War Diary	Trepied		11/01/1917	11/01/1917
War Diary	Aix-en-Issart		11/01/1917	11/01/1917
War Diary	Trepied		12/01/1917	12/01/1917
War Diary	Aix-en-Issart		12/01/1917	12/01/1917
War Diary	Trepied		13/01/1917	13/01/1917
War Diary	Aix-en-Issart		13/01/1917	13/01/1917
War Diary	Trepied		14/01/1917	14/01/1917
War Diary	Manesquel		14/01/1917	14/01/1917
War Diary	Trepied		15/01/1917	16/01/1917
War Diary	Mulimont Plage		16/01/1917	16/01/1917
War Diary	Trepied		17/01/1917	19/01/1917
War Diary	Bahot Peits Berrantto		19/01/1917	19/01/1917
War Diary	Trepied		20/01/1917	20/01/1917
War Diary	Mulimont Plage		20/01/1917	20/01/1917
War Diary	Trepied		21/01/1917	21/01/1917
War Diary	Puits Berrantto		21/01/1917	21/01/1917
War Diary	Trepied		22/01/1917	22/01/1917
War Diary	Fruges		22/01/1917	22/01/1917
War Diary	Trepied		23/01/1917	25/01/1917
War Diary	St Josse		25/01/1917	25/01/1917
War Diary	Trepied		26/01/1917	26/01/1917

War Diary	Irepied	26/01/1917	26/01/1917
War Diary	Trepied	27/01/1917	27/01/1917
War Diary	Aubin St Vaast	27/01/1917	27/01/1917
War Diary	Trepied	28/01/1917	29/01/1917
War Diary	Irepied	29/01/1917	29/01/1917
War Diary	Trepied	30/01/1917	30/01/1917
War Diary	Fruges	31/01/1917	31/01/1917
War Diary	Trepied	31/01/1917	31/01/1917
Heading	War Diary of No. 12 Sanitary Section 2nd London Sanitary Company R.A.M.C.T.F. For January 1917		
Heading	War Diary of No. 12 Sanitary Section 2nd London Sanitary Company R.A.M.C. T.F. February 1917		
War Diary	Trepied	01/02/1917	03/02/1917
War Diary	Beauvainville	03/02/1917	03/02/1917
War Diary	Trepied	04/02/1917	08/02/1917
War Diary	Frgesite	08/02/1917	08/02/1917
War Diary	Trepied	09/02/1917	23/02/1917
War Diary	Berhe	23/02/1917	23/02/1917
War Diary	Trepied	24/02/1917	25/02/1917
War Diary	Irepied	26/02/1917	26/02/1917
War Diary	St Josse	26/02/1917	26/02/1917
War Diary	Trepied	27/02/1917	27/02/1917
War Diary	Renty	27/02/1917	27/02/1917
War Diary	Trepied	28/02/1917	28/02/1917
Heading	War Diary of No. 12 Sanitary Section 2nd London Sanitary Company R.A.M.C.T.F. February 1917		
Heading	War Diary of No. 12 Sanitary Section 2nd London Sanitary R.A.M.C.T. March 1917		
War Diary	Trepied	01/03/1917	01/03/1917
War Diary	Aix-en-Issart	01/03/1917	01/03/1917
War Diary	Trepied	02/03/1917	02/03/1917
War Diary	Les Piuts Bernault	02/03/1917	02/03/1917
War Diary	Trepied	03/03/1917	03/03/1917
War Diary	Les Puits Bernault	03/03/1917	03/03/1917
War Diary	Renty	03/03/1917	03/03/1917
War Diary	Trepied	04/03/1917	04/03/1917
War Diary	Compigneulles-Les-Petites	04/03/1917	05/03/1917
War Diary	Trepied	05/03/1917	05/03/1917
War Diary	Merimont Cueq	05/03/1917	05/03/1917
War Diary	Trepied	06/03/1917	06/03/1917
War Diary	Verton	06/03/1917	06/03/1917
War Diary	Trepied	07/03/1917	07/03/1917
War Diary	Bois Jean	07/03/1917	07/03/1917
War Diary	Trepied	08/03/1917	08/03/1917
War Diary	St Denoux	08/03/1917	08/03/1917
War Diary	Campigneulles	08/03/1917	08/03/1917
War Diary	Trepied	09/03/1917	09/03/1917
War Diary	Embry	09/03/1917	09/03/1917
War Diary	Beauvainville	09/03/1917	09/03/1917
War Diary	Trepied	10/03/1917	10/03/1917
War Diary	Campaign	10/03/1917	10/03/1917
War Diary	Trepied	11/03/1917	11/03/1917
War Diary	Beauvainville	11/03/1917	11/03/1917
War Diary	Trepied	12/03/1917	12/03/1917
War Diary	Beauvainville	12/03/1917	12/03/1917
War Diary	Marles	12/03/1917	12/03/1917

Type	Location	Date From	Date To
War Diary	Trepied	13/03/1917	13/03/1917
War Diary	Aix-en-Issart	13/03/1917	13/03/1917
War Diary	Puits Berrantto	13/03/1917	13/03/1917
War Diary	Trepied	14/03/1917	14/03/1917
War Diary	Aix-en-Issart	14/03/1917	14/03/1917
War Diary	Maresquel	14/03/1917	14/03/1917
War Diary	Trepied	15/03/1917	15/03/1917
War Diary	Irepied	15/03/1917	15/03/1917
War Diary	Trepied	16/03/1917	16/03/1917
War Diary	Aix-en-Issart	16/03/1917	16/03/1917
War Diary	Merles & Marant	16/03/1917	16/03/1917
War Diary	Offin	16/03/1917	16/03/1917
War Diary	Trepied	17/03/1917	17/03/1917
War Diary	Offin	17/03/1917	17/03/1917
War Diary	Trepied	17/03/1917	18/03/1917
War Diary	Lassin & Beaurain	18/03/1917	18/03/1917
War Diary	Trepied	19/03/1917	19/03/1917
War Diary	Aubin-St-Vaast	19/03/1917	19/03/1917
War Diary	Aix-en-Issart	19/03/1917	19/03/1917
War Diary	Trepied	20/03/1917	20/03/1917
War Diary	Plumoison	20/03/1917	20/03/1917
War Diary	Fvessin	20/03/1917	20/03/1917
War Diary	Trepied	21/03/1917	21/03/1917
War Diary	Irepied	21/03/1917	21/03/1917
War Diary	Trepied	22/03/1917	22/03/1917
War Diary	Rimboval	22/03/1917	22/03/1917
War Diary	Irepied	23/03/1917	23/03/1917
War Diary	Lebech & Toray	23/03/1917	23/03/1917
War Diary	Verton	23/03/1917	23/03/1917
War Diary	Trepied	24/03/1917	24/03/1917
War Diary	Creqy	24/03/1917	24/03/1917
War Diary	Trepied	25/03/1917	25/03/1917
War Diary	Fruges	25/03/1917	25/03/1917
War Diary	Trepied	26/03/1917	26/03/1917
War Diary	Coupelle Vielle	26/03/1917	26/03/1917
War Diary	Trepied	27/03/1917	27/03/1917
War Diary	Coupelle Neure & Fruges	27/03/1917	27/03/1917
War Diary	St Josse	27/03/1917	27/03/1917
War Diary	Trepied	28/03/1917	28/03/1917
War Diary	Campignulles Les Grands	28/03/1917	28/03/1917
War Diary	Trepied	29/03/1917	31/03/1917
War Diary	Lepinoy Maresquel Plumoison	31/03/1917	31/03/1917
Heading	War Diary of No. 12 Sanitary Section of The 2nd London Sanitary Co R.A.M.C.T. March 1-1-17		
Heading	3rd Cav. Div. War Diary For April 1917 No 12 Sanitary Section 2nd London Sanitary Co R.A.M.C.T.		
War Diary	Trepied	01/04/1917	05/04/1917
War Diary	Maresquel	05/04/1917	07/04/1917
War Diary	Monchel	07/04/1917	08/04/1917
War Diary	Gour-en-Artois	08/04/1917	10/04/1917
War Diary	Arras	11/04/1917	11/04/1917
War Diary	Gouy-en-Artois	12/04/1917	16/04/1917
War Diary	Wavans	16/04/1917	19/04/1917
War Diary	Rossignol	20/04/1917	26/04/1917
War Diary	Herdin	27/04/1917	27/04/1917
War Diary	Lepinoye	27/04/1917	27/04/1917

War Diary	Maresquel	27/04/1917	27/04/1917
War Diary	Dompierre	28/04/1917	28/04/1917
War Diary	Wadicourt	28/04/1917	28/04/1917
War Diary	Vivonchamy	28/04/1917	28/04/1917
War Diary	Vron	28/04/1917	28/04/1917
War Diary	Creg	28/04/1917	28/04/1917
War Diary	Rossignol	29/04/1917	29/04/1917
War Diary	Nempont	29/04/1917	29/04/1917
War Diary	Pt Preux	29/04/1917	29/04/1917
War Diary	Rossignol	30/04/1917	30/04/1917
Heading	War Diary For April 1917 No.12 Sanitary Section 2nd London Sanitary Co R.A.M.C.T.		
Heading	War Diary For May 1917 2nd London Sanitary Company R.A.M.C.T. No.12 Section 3rd Cavalry Division		
War Diary	Escveis les Cregy	01/05/1917	01/05/1917
War Diary	Le Petit Rossignol Le Petit Chemin	02/05/1917	02/05/1917
War Diary	Raye	03/05/1917	03/05/1917
War Diary	Ligincourt	03/05/1917	03/05/1917
War Diary	Rossignol	04/05/1917	05/05/1917
War Diary	Etables	05/05/1917	05/05/1917
War Diary	Regnauville	06/05/1917	06/05/1917
War Diary	Maintenay	06/05/1917	06/05/1917
War Diary	Dominois Le Petit Chemin	07/05/1917	07/05/1917
War Diary	?	08/05/1917	08/05/1917
War Diary	Bois Jean	08/05/1917	08/05/1917
War Diary	Naaintenay	08/05/1917	08/05/1917
War Diary	Dominois	08/05/1917	08/05/1917
War Diary	Torte Fontaine	08/05/1917	08/05/1917
War Diary	Dompierre	08/05/1917	08/05/1917
War Diary	Newport	09/05/1917	09/05/1917
War Diary	Muntin	09/05/1917	09/05/1917
War Diary	Grand Preux	09/05/1917	09/05/1917
War Diary	Clabend Romatt	09/05/1917	09/05/1917
War Diary	Lepinoy	09/05/1917	09/05/1917
War Diary	Beauvainville	09/05/1917	09/05/1917
War Diary	Aubrin St Vaast	09/05/1917	09/05/1917
War Diary	Newport Eumin	10/05/1917	10/05/1917
War Diary	Tortefontaine	11/05/1917	11/05/1917
War Diary	Borriquel	12/05/1917	12/05/1917
War Diary	Wavans	13/05/1917	13/05/1917
War Diary	Tincourt	14/05/1917	14/05/1917
War Diary	Pevoune	15/05/1917	15/05/1917
War Diary	Tincourt	16/05/1917	17/05/1917
War Diary	Convelles	17/05/1917	17/05/1917
War Diary	Tincourt	18/05/1917	20/05/1917
War Diary	Catelet	20/05/1917	20/05/1917
War Diary	Tincourt	21/05/1917	26/05/1917
War Diary	Embry	26/05/1917	26/05/1917
War Diary	Tincourt	26/05/1917	27/05/1917
War Diary	Embry	28/05/1917	28/05/1917
War Diary	Tincourt	29/05/1917	31/05/1917
Heading	War Diary For May 1917 No 12 Sanitary Section 2nd London Sanitary Company R.A.M.C.T. 3rd Cavalry Division		

Heading	War Diary For June 1917 No 12 Sanitary Section 2nd London Sanitary Co R.A.M.C.T.		
War Diary	Tincourt	01/06/1917	01/06/1917
War Diary	Embry	01/06/1917	01/06/1917
War Diary	Tincourt	02/06/1917	02/06/1917
War Diary	Baiuse	03/06/1917	03/06/1917
War Diary	Tincourt	04/06/1917	04/06/1917
War Diary	Baiuse	05/06/1917	05/06/1917
War Diary	Tincourt	06/06/1917	30/06/1917

WO 95/1149/1

B.E.F. FRANCE & FLANDERS.
3 CAVALRY DIV. TROOPS.
12 SANITARY SECTION.
1915 JAN TO 1917 JUNE.
13 MOBILE VETERINARY
    SECTION.
1914 OCT TO 1919 APR.
14 MOB VETERINARY SECTION
1914 OCT TO 1919 MAY.
20 MOB VETERINARY SECTION
1915 MAR TO 1918 FEB.

B.E.F. FRANCE & FLANDERS.
3 CAVALRY DIV. TROOPS.
12 SANITARY SECTION.
1915 JAN TO 1917 JUNE.
13 MOBILE VETERINARY
            SECTION.
1914 OCT TO 1919 APR.
14 MOB VETERINARY SECTION
1914 OCT TO 1919 MAY.
20 MOB VETERINARY SECTION
1915 MAR TO 1918 FEB.

1149

1915-1916
3RD CAVALRY DIVISION

NO. 12 SANITARY SECTION

JAN 1915 - ~~DEC 1916~~
JUNE 1917

121/4327
Jan. 1915

Summarised but not copied

Wt. No 12. Sanitary section 2nd Cavy Division

Vol I.

Jan 1915 — Dec 1916

1. Sanitary Section, III Cav. Div.

WAR DIARY
of
INTELLIGENCE SUMMARY.
(Erase heading not required.)

Army Form C. 2118.

Instructions regarding War Diaries and Intelligence Summaries are contained in F.S. Regs., Part II and the Staff Manual respectively. Title pages will be prepared in manuscript.

[Stamp: SANITARY SECTION — THIRD CAVALRY DVN.]

Hour, Date, Place	Summary of Events and Information	Remarks and references to Appendices
January 11th 1915. Hazebrouck	Built latrine & dug urine pit for 4th K. Co. A.S.C. where men had been evacuating on roadside even. Incinerator built at back of Hôtel de Ville for 56th Co A.S.C. Two men made inspection of billets, finding filthy conditions prevailing such as:— (a) Privy opening out of a dairy. (b) Billets adjoining officers quarters in filthy condition. (c) Stable used as billet, with stable yard only 3' away	
12th. Hazebrouck	Built badly needed incinerator for 16th. Co. Also a brick incinerator.	
Hazebrouck	Inspection of 12th. Signal Squadron billets which were in fair order.	
13th. Hazebrouck	Buried unsound fruit on private property; dangerous to health of surrounding billets. Brick incinerator. Disinfection of supply van.	

WAR DIARY / INTELLIGENCE SUMMARY

Sanitary Section, III Cavalry Division

Army Form C. 2118.

(Erase heading not required.)

Hour, Date, Place	Summary of Events and Information	Remarks and references to Appendices
January 14th 1915 Mondycken Morbecque	Sanitary inspection of billets of Leicester, R.H.A. + ammunition Col. Sanitary work needed.	
	Obtained disinfector at 16th A.S.C. not being used regularly. Incinerator built which see envelope in main road.	
15th Morbecque Hazebrouck	Disinfection of 2 lorries. Latrines + urine pits, one of latter for 16 C. officers. Joined adpt at Q.M.G's H.Q. Rubbish burned at A.D.M.S's quarters Inspected Essex Y. camp. Advised on to isolation of chicken pox. Went to Lieut Benquin but did not see 10th Hussars as to cleanliness.	
16th Hazebrouck	Finished brick incinerator in yard of hospital near post office. Made brick gate for bath there.	

3. Sanitary Section, 3rd Cavalry Div. **WAR DIARY** or **INTELLIGENCE SUMMARY**
(Erase heading not required.)

Army Form C. 2118.

Instructions regarding War Diaries and Intelligence Summaries are contained in F.S. Regs., Part II and the Staff Manual respectively. Title pages will be prepared in manuscript.

SANITARY SECTION
No. 3
Date.
THIRD CAVALRY DIV.

Hour, Date, Place	Summary of Events and Information	Remarks and references to Appendices
January 18th. 1915. Hondeghem	Inspection of billets, premises. Selecting sites for incinerators & latrines. Removal of large accumulation of manure. Consultation with Col. McKerrill re bathing and washing, and as to form of clothes.	
January 19th. Hondeghem	Seeing to case of enteric with refugee child. Continuation of previous day's sanitation.	
January 20th. Hondeghem	Erection of urine pit & latrines with screen round the same. Emptying of dung pit. Making of four dung mounds. Cleaning of water courses.	
January 21st. Hondeghem	Inspection of billets of Essex Yeomanry at Le Bois and reporting of same to A.D.M.S. Cleaning out manure pit. Loading bricks and making of two incinerators.	CAM

WAR DIARY
or
INTELLIGENCE SUMMARY.

(Erase heading not required.)

Army Form C. 2118.

Instructions regarding War Diaries and Intelligence Summaries are contained in F. S. Regs., Part II and the Staff Manual respectively. Title pages will be prepared in manuscript.

SANITARY SECTION
No. 4
THIRD CAVALRY DIVN.

Hour, Date, Place	Summary of Events and Information	Remarks and references to Appendices
January 22nd 1915 Hooglede Hazebrouck	Carting bricks for two incinerators and building of the same. Removal of farm refuse & manure	
23rd. Hooglede	Building of two incinerators + removal of refuse.	
25th. Vieux Berquin/Strazeele	Inspection of billets of 10th. Hussars. Disinfection of manure of Lace factory in rue du Pré where are billeted 300 R.E. signallers.	CAW
Strazeele	Building of incinerators + removal of refuse. Inspection of billets.	aw.
26th. Hazebrouck Hondeghem	Disinfection with care of measles among H.Q. grooms. Removal of refuse + building of incinerators.	
27th. Hazebrouck	"C" Battery R.H.A., measles disinfection. Inspection by I.M. Sir John French.	CAW

(7.3989) W4141—463. 400,000. 9/14. H.&J.Ltd. Forms/C. 2118/10.

Army Form C. 2118.

WAR DIARY
or
INTELLIGENCE SUMMARY.

(Erase heading not required.)

Instructions regarding War Diaries and Intelligence Summaries are contained in F.S. Regs., Part II and the Staff Manual respectively. Title pages will be prepared in manuscript.

SANITARY SECTION
No. 5
THIRD CAVALRY DIV.

Hour, Date, Place	Summary of Events and Information	Remarks and references to Appendices
JANUARY		
28th. Hazebrouck	Further disinfection with case of measles among H.Q. grooms	
29th. Hazebrouck	General routine.	
30th. Hazebrouck	Inspection of billet of A.O.C. General routine.	
31st. Hazebrouck	General routine.	

Culverwell

Summarised but not copied

No. 12. Sanctuary Section. 3rd Cavalry Division

Vol II

Army Form C. 2118.

WAR DIARY
or
INTELLIGENCE SUMMARY.
(Erase heading not required.)

Instructions regarding War Diaries and Intelligence Summaries are contained in F.S. Regs., Part II and the Staff Manual respectively. Title pages will be prepared in manuscript.

[STAMP: SANITARY SECTION / THIRD CAVALRY DIV / No. / Date]

Hour, Date, Place	Summary of Events and Information	Remarks and references to Appendices
FEBRUARY		
1st Hazebrouck	General routine.	
2nd Hazebrouck	Inspection of R.E. Signallers Billets.	
3rd Hazebrouck	General routine.	
4th Hazebrouck	General routine.	
5th	Taking up quarters in YPRES	
6th Ypres	Cleaning Divisional headquarters.	
	Digging latrines & manure pit. Running refuse of quarters 10 h. Ground too frozen.	
7th Ypres	Continuation of previous days work. Clawson	

Army Form C. 2118.

WAR DIARY
or
INTELLIGENCE SUMMARY.
(Erase heading not required.)

SANITARY SECTION
THIRD CAVALRY DIV.

Hour, Date, Place	Summary of Events and Information	Remarks and references to Appendices
FEBRUARY 8TH YPRES	Continuation of burial of refuse & digging latrines at Divisional Headquarters. CRW	
9TH YPRES	Burying refuse at H.Q. Erection of baths at H.Q. Bathing of 10th Hussars, Essex Yeomanry & Life Guards. CRW	
10TH, 11TH	Continuation of same. CRW	
12TH	Return to HAZEBROUCK. CRW	
13TH HAZEB'K	General routine. CRW	
14TH HAZEB'K	Inspection of cesspool of No.5 Motor Ambulance Convoy. General routine. CRW	
15TH HAZEB'K	Disinfection of billets of R.E. Signallers & A.O.C. CRW	
16TH HAZEB'K	General routine.	
17TH	Disinfection of Detention House, III Cavalry Division — vermin suspected house. Disinfection of Blankets, tuberculosis case. CRW	

Army Form C. 2118.

WAR DIARY
or
INTELLIGENCE SUMMARY.
(Erase heading not required.)

Instructions regarding War Diaries and Intelligence Summaries are contained in F.S. Regs., Part II and the Staff Manual respectively. Title pages will be prepared in manuscript.

Hour, Date, Place	Summary of Events and Information	Remarks and references to Appendices
18th February HAZEBROUCK	Inspection & reporting on B Echelon stables.	
19th "	Disinfection of bedding from Headquarters Details billet. Case of lice.	
20th "	Periodical cleaning of own billet. CWW	
21st "	General routine.	
22nd "	General routine.	
23rd "	Clearing of yard & making incinerator & latrines at B Echelon. Cau.	
24th "	Continuation of work at B Echelon. Latrine pits at B Echelon stables. Supervision of baths for dismounted troops at Gasworks. Cau.	

WAR DIARY
or
INTELLIGENCE SUMMARY.

Army Form C. 2118.

(*Erase heading not required.*)

Instructions regarding War Diaries and Intelligence Summaries are contained in F.S. Regs., Part II and the Staff Manual respectively. Title pages will be prepared in manuscript.

SANITARY SECTION No. 9 THIRD CAVALRY DIV.

Hour, Date, Place	Summary of Events and Information	Remarks and references to Appendices
FEBRUARY		
25TH. HAZEBROUCK.	"B" Echelon. Going around latrines & superintending cleaning of gardens. Inspecting men's quarters. Cav.	
26TH.	Supervision of latrines, 70 men bathed. Cav. Inspection of billets, incinerators, etc. of 43 & 96 Columns A.S.C. Cav.	
27TH.	Supervising booths. " Cav.	
28TH.	Disinfection of blankets from A Echelon & Y.M.C.A.. General routine. Cav.	

12/4893
March 1915

13/4893.

Summarised but not copied

6012. Sanitary Section. 3rd Cavalry Division

Vol III

Army Form C. 2118.

WAR DIARY
or
INTELLIGENCE SUMMARY.
(Erase heading not required.)

Instructions regarding War Diaries and Intelligence Summaries are contained in F.S. Regs., Part II and the Staff Manual respectively. Title pages will be prepared in manuscript.

[Stamp: SANITARY SECTION, No. 1, Date MARCH 1/15, THIRD CAVALRY DIV.]

Hour, Date, Place	Summary of Events and Information	Remarks and references to Appendices
MARCH 1. Hazebrouck	Superintending baths at Garrawets (10th. Hussars) Disinfection at 'B' Echelon quarters	
Strazeele	Disinfection of Blankets by Lt. Life Guards (Oneil) A.g.e.	
2. Ebblinghem	Disinfector with "Dancel" disinfector of blankets of 1st. Life Guards. Baths at Garrawets, Staywrich. Disinfection continued.	
3. "	do.	
Staywrick	Superintending baths.	CMM
4. "	Water Ambulance Column, Spray disinfection (meningitis)	
Steenbecque	4th Somerset Yeomanry: Disinfection of billets (Suspected meningitis)	CMM
Ebblingham	Bree disinfector used for blankets of 1st. Life Guards.	
Staywrick	'Dancel' disinfector with 4th. O.C.	
5.	Instructing 'B' Lachelen in use of 'Silli' water cart. Instructing water party, 10th. Hussars in use of Horse V (Chlorine) water cart.	CMM

Army Form C. 2118.

WAR DIARY
or
INTELLIGENCE SUMMARY.
(Erase heading not required.)

Instructions regarding War Diaries and Intelligence Summaries are contained in F.S. Regs., Part II and the Staff Manual respectively. Title pages will be prepared in manuscript.

Hour, Date, Place	Summary of Events and Information	Remarks and references to Appendices
March 6. Steenbecque	"Thresh" disinfector used with Gooch Saunders Manouvin. General routine.	It was found that though the Source was clear, on a sample Chloride was not sufficient to disinfect fifty gallons. On start on breakfast. This example was found to be just sufficient.
7. Hazebrouck		
8. "	Drinking water passed through "Horrocks" Sterliser. do.	
9. & 10. "	Disinfectors used at Steenbecque & Hazebrouck. do.	The test used was as follows: 2 c.c. of ½ saturated starch sol. were mixed with 50 c.c. of the water. The amount of ½% sodium hypochlorite which gave a colour the same as that in the first case & only gave so in the second. It was found previously that one drop of which would render some conditions small pieces of chlorine in 2000 to 4000 Salt solution of chloride of lime.
11. "	Standing to.	
12. & 13. "	of M.A.C.	
	Standing to. Repairs to drainage of billets of officers	
14. & 15. "	General routine. Repairs to drainage of billets of S.[?] quarters	
16. "	Cleaning of A.P.M. headquarters.	
17. "		
Serve	10-a. Inadons: Inspection with subfield one.	
Hazebrouck.	Disinfection of worn blankets. Repetition boil pump at Deletion House Superintending baths.	

WAR DIARY
or
INTELLIGENCE SUMMARY.
(Erase heading not required.)

Army Form C. 2118.

Instructions regarding War Diaries and Intelligence Summaries are contained in F.S. Regs., Part II and the Staff Manual respectively. Title pages will be prepared in manuscript.

SANITARY SECTION
No. 3
Date 1 Mar S.S. 15
THIRD CAVALRY DIV.

Hour, Date, Place	Summary of Events and Information	Remarks and references to Appendices
MARCH 18. Borsbeeck	General routine.	
19. "	Constructing new water cart at A.D.M.S.	Cau
20. Borsbeek	General routine.	Cau
21. Hazebrouck	Inspected 'A' Echelon – suspected case of meningitis.	
22. "	General routine.	Cau
23. Ettlingem	"	Cau
" Hazebrouck	"Sireul" disinfector with 1st Life Guards. Superintending baths.	
24. "	Baths & disinfection, as before.	Cau
25. "	Cleaning offices of Divisional Headquarters and advising on water supply.	
26. "	Do.	
27. "	Demonstrating water cart to A.S.C.	

WAR DIARY
or
INTELLIGENCE SUMMARY.

(Erase heading not required.)

Army Form C. 2118.

SANITARY SECTION
No. 4
Date MARCH 15
THIRD CAVALRY DIV.

Hour, Date, Place	Summary of Events and Information	Remarks and references to Appendices
March 28. Hazebrouck	Inspecting billets of F.C.B.O. Advising re isolation & disinfection, milk, case of scarlet fever.	
29. Hondeghem	Inspection of Brigade Vermorel killers & water cart.	
30. "	Instruction of " " water party.	
31. "	do and testing water	
Steenberge	Inspection & instructing re & isolation of case of measles.	
	Repairing Field water cart pump.	
Hazebrouck	Baths	Cecil

Summarised but not copied

No. 12. Sang: Section. 3rd Aus: Division

Vol IV

12/5/1915

12/15/15
April 2nd 1915

S
April 1915

Army Form C. 2118.

WAR DIARY
or
INTELLIGENCE SUMMARY.

(Erase heading not required.)

SANITARY SECTION — THIRD CAVALRY DIV.
No. 1/5/91

Instructions regarding War Diaries and Intelligence Summaries are contained in F.S. Regs., Part II and the Staff Manual respectively. Title pages will be prepared in manuscript.

Hour, Date, Place	Summary of Events and Information	Remarks and references to Appendices
April 1st Haybrouck	Rectifying sanitation at R.Q.M.s Supervision of Baths for our troops at Cassell	
" 2nd Ellingham	Water tests at H.Q. 7th C Bde.	
Haybrouck	Supervision of Baths	
" 3rd Ellingham	Work at 8th Brigade H.Q.	
Haybrouck	Supervision of Baths	
" 4th "	General Routine	
" 5th "	General Routine	
" 6th Morbecque	Water Cart examination E.F.C.O.	
" 4th "	Inspection & advice re crew of Shell at Supply Col.	
Haybrouck	Inspection of billets of 2nd & 7th Bde. Disinfection of blankets from Ed. Echelon Supervision of Baths.	

Claviston

Army Form C. 2118.

WAR DIARY
or
INTELLIGENCE SUMMARY.
(Erase heading not required.)

Instructions regarding War Diaries and Intelligence Summaries are contained in F. S. Regs., Part II and the Staff Manual respectively. Title pages will be prepared in manuscript.

SANITARY SECTION
No. 1/3/1915
THIRD CAVALRY DIV.

Hour, Date, Place	Summary of Events and Information	Remarks and references to Appendices
April 9th Moncheaux	Instructions in water duties R.A.M.C.	
" Keyhem	Disinfectors of Blatton filter	
" "	" " Henry Douvrin	
" "	Supervision of Bath	
9th Leven	Instructing Sanitary Squad 4/1st R Kumaon	
10th "	" " " " " "	
11th Keyhem	Disinfecting blankets of North Somerset Yeomanry	
" "	General Routine	
12th Moncheaux	Inspection of Ent. Homebleux & nets. Yeomanry	
13th Legende	Steam Disinfecting at Essex Yeomanry	
" Renescure	Inspection of district re suspected cases	
14th Moncheaux	Inspection of billets Landana	
" Keyhem	" " re: cart of donkies	
	Inspection of Bath	

(7·599) W4141—463. 400,000. 9/14. H.&J.Ltd. Forms/C. 2118/10.

WAR DIARY or INTELLIGENCE SUMMARY.

Army Form C. 2118.

(Erase heading not required.)

Hour, Date, Place	Summary of Events and Information	Remarks and references to Appendices
April 15 Lydd	Sanitary squad at work	
" " " Seven	Disinfection Wm at Eros Germany	
" " "	Instructing sanitary squad of 15th Hussars	
" 16 Hazybrouck	Disinfection at B. Echelon	
" " "	Supervision of Baths	
" " Lydd	Sanitary squad at Lynne, R.H.E's	
" 17th "	Disinfection at Lynne	
" " Hazybrouck	General Rantin	
" 18 Steenkerque	Disinfection of Billets, seven cases of Measles	
" " Lydd	Sanitary squad at work	
" 19 Steenkerque	Disinfection of Billets	
" " Lydd	Sanitary squad at work R.H.E's	
" 20 "	Sanitary " " "	
	Sanitary General Rantin	Cawston

WAR DIARY
or
INTELLIGENCE SUMMARY.
(Erase heading not required.)

Army Form C. 2118.

Sanitary Section, Third Cavalry Division — 1/5/1915

Hour, Date, Place	Summary of Events and Information	Remarks and references to Appendices
April 21st Hazebrouck Lynde	Disinfection at R.P.M's. Supervision of Baths. Sanitary squad at work.	
22nd Wallon Cappel Hazebrouck	Steam disinfection at 2nd L.Dr. Supervision of Baths.	
23rd "	Received orders to stand by, ready to move off.	
24th "	Standing by.	
25th "	Standing by.	
26th "	Disinfection at No. 5 Clearing Hospital. Disinfection at Lynde stable.	
27th "	Incinerate bedding and disinfection at No. 5 Clearing Hospital.	

WAR DIARY of **INTELLIGENCE SUMMARY.**

Army Form C. 2118.

(Erase heading not required.)

SANITARY SECTION — THIRD CAVALRY DIV. — 1/5/915

Hour, Date, Place	Summary of Events and Information	Remarks and references to Appendices
April 28th Hargicourt	Disinfecting and cleaning out ditches.	
"	Disinfecting Horse & Brown kit, also Ambulance.	
Montecque	Cleaning out choked drain and cesspool	
29th "	Disinfecting Horse and Brown.	
Hargicourt	Disinfecting Horses and Brown & kit.	
" "	Disinfecting Roadway occupied by Ammunition Park Northumbrian Div.	
" "	Disinfect Ambulance & brown & kit	
30th "	Disinfecting and Incinerator building at No. 5 Clearing Hospital	
" "	Disinfecting Blankets & kit of 76th Amm. Col.	

Cameron

12/5546

May 1915.

S/

Recommended but not acted

3rd Cavalry Division

No 12. Sanitary Section

Vol V

12/5546

WAR DIARY
or
INTELLIGENCE SUMMARY.
(Erase heading not required.)

Army Form C. 2118.

Instructions regarding War Diaries and Intelligence Summaries are contained in F.S. Regs., Part II and the Staff Manual respectively. Title pages will be prepared in manuscript.

Hour, Date, Place	Summary of Events and Information	Remarks and references to Appendices
Hazebrouck 1st May 1915.	Party cleaning & disinfecting at South Midland Clearing hospital. Inspection of Officers Mess as above. Supervision of Baths.	
Hazebrouck 2/5/15.	General Routine.	
" 3rd May	Party cleaning & disinfecting at St Mil. Hos. Supervision of Baths. Rec'd orders to stand by ready to move off. Party disinfecting billets, cases sent to hospital meningitis.	
" 4th May	General Routine. Moving by to	
" 5th May	Party cleaning & disinfecting at St Midland Hos. Sanitary Inspection at D.M. Supervision of Baths.	

WAR DIARY
or
INTELLIGENCE SUMMARY.
(Erase heading not required.)

Army Form C. 2118.

Hour, Date, Place	Summary of Events and Information	Remarks and references to Appendices
Scarborough 6th	Party at South Midland Hospital.	
" 7th May	Party at " " " "	
" "	Party disinfecting at No 10. Cas. Clg.Station	
8th May	Party at South Midland Hospital	
" "	Sanitary Inspection of Town	
9th May	Party removing stumming refuse from rear of N° Such Hosp.	
" "	Whole Section at B Echelon making hocks.	
10th May	General Routine.	
" "	Supervision of Baths.	
" "	Sanitary Inspection of Town.	
11th May	Party disinfecting at No 10.C.C.S.	
" "	Supervision of Bath.	

CRM

Army Form C. 2118.

WAR DIARY
or
INTELLIGENCE SUMMARY.
(Erase heading not required.)

Instructions regarding War Diaries and Intelligence Summaries are contained in F.S. Regs., Part II and the Staff Manual respectively. Title pages will be prepared in manuscript.

Hour, Date, Place	Summary of Events and Information	Remarks and references to Appendices
Hazebrouck 11th May	A.D. "Vidange" Men (Attached) Emptying Cesspools at No 10 C.C.S	
" " "	Sanitary Inspection of Town.	
12th May	Disinfecting Party at No 10 CCS	
" " "	Supervision of Baths.	
" " "	Emptying Cesspools at N. Mid Hospital	
" " "	Sanitary Inspection of Town.	
13th May	Disinfection at No 10 CCS	
" " "	Supervision of Baths.	
" " "	Emptying Cesspools at N. Mid Hospital.	
" " "	Sanitary Inspection of Town.	
" " "	Disinfecting billet after case of Measles	
14th May	Disinfecting Party at No 10 C.C.S.	
" " "	Emptying Cesspools at billets of N. Mid Hosp.	
" " "	Sanitary Inspection of Town.	CAU

Army Form C. 2118.

WAR DIARY
or
INTELLIGENCE SUMMARY.
(Erase heading not required.)

Instructions regarding War Diaries and Intelligence Summaries are contained in F.S. Regs., Part II and the Staff Manual respectively. Title pages will be prepared in manuscript.

Hour, Date, Place	Summary of Events and Information	Remarks and references to Appendices
Headquarters of	Party at No 10 C.Cd.	
15th May	Employing breakfast at Q.M. O. Headquarters also the 1 Shropshire D. Block.	
"	Sanitary Inspection of town	
16th May	Received Ambulance of 1 Coy at Depot.	
"	Clearing away refuse at killer of P.O.W.	
"	Disinfection party at No 10 C.Cd.	
17th May	Officers & 18 men evacuated to hourd 35.	
"	Party cleaning at 2. Mid Hospital.	
"	Party instructing in sanitation at A.b.o	
"	Motor Bus Col.	
"	Disinfecting party at No 10 CCd	
"	Emptying Dustbins at Gen. H.Q. South Midland CCS. Sanitary inspection of town	

(73989) W4141—463. 400,000. 9/14. H.&J.,Ltd. Forms/C. 2118/10.

Army Form C. 2118.

WAR DIARY
or
INTELLIGENCE SUMMARY.
(Erase heading not required.)

Instructions regarding War Diaries and Intelligence Summaries are contained in F.S. Regs., Part II and the Staff Manual respectively. Title pages will be prepared in manuscript.

Hour, Date, Place	Summary of Events and Information	Remarks and references to Appendices
Haystruck. 18th May	Supervision of Baths. Emptying cesspools at No 10 ccd also at Motor ambulance Convoy. Inspection of Town.	
" " "		
Point 35. " "	General Routine.	
Haystruck 19th May	General Routine.	
Point 35. 19th "	Inspecting & cleaning up Bivouac ground occupied by 6th 7th & 8th Can. Fd amb & 6th 7th & 8th Bdes	
Haystruck. 20th May	Sanitary inspection of Town.	
Point 35 20th "	Inspecting & cleaning up Bivouacs as above.	
Haystruck 21st "	Emptying cesspools at Telegraph Office. Collecting horse manure from the Church &c. General Staff Headquarters. San: inspection of Town.	
Point 35 21st "	Cleaning up Bivouac grounds as above.	
Haystruck. 22nd "	General Routine. Officers' men returned from Point 35. Casu	

Army Form C. 2118.

WAR DIARY
or
INTELLIGENCE SUMMARY.
(Erase heading not required.)

Instructions regarding War Diaries and Intelligence Summaries are contained in F.S. Regs., Part II and the Staff Manual respectively. Title pages will be prepared in manuscript.

Hour, Date, Place	Summary of Events and Information	Remarks and references to Appendices
Hazebrouck 23rd May	General Routine.	
" 24th May	General Routine.	
" 25th May	General Routine. Supervision of Baths.	
" 26th May	Rec'd orders for Officers & 2 3rd Corps to Renescure	
" 26th "	Supervision of Baths. 1 NCO & 3 men remain at Hazebrouck.	
Renescure 27th "	O.C. at Can Corps Supply Col. re suspected case of Enteric. General Routine.	
" " 27th "	Enteric. General Routine.	
" " 27th "	Party Cleaning up, digging latrines at Hd Qrtrs.	
Hazebrouck 27th "	Supervision of Baths.	
Renescure 28th May	General Routine. Taking notes &c.	
" " 29th "	Party left for disinfection at Cambrigne 2nd/30 Bt.	
" " 29th "	Rec'd orders for Officers & 44 men to proceed	
" " "	to Vlamertinghe.	
Vlamertinghe 30th May	Party disinfecting at Hd Qrtrs billets, also	
" 30th "	Cleaning yard in front of dressing station.	
" 30th "	Cleaning House used as Mortuary, infectious Ward &c.	

(73959) W4141-463. 400,000. 9/14. H.&J.,Ltd. Forms/C. 2118/10.

WAR DIARY
or
INTELLIGENCE SUMMARY.

(Erase heading not required.)

Army Form C. 2118.

Hour, Date, Place	Summary of Events and Information	Remarks and references to Appendices
Ontd. Vlamertinghe 30th May	Cleaning & disinfecting Sanitary Off: Billets.	
" 3rd "	Cleaning & disinfecting Wards at Advanced Dressing Station Ypres.	
" 31st May	Disinfecting rubbish heaps and cleaning up at Advanced Dressing Station Ypres.	
" 3rd "	Inspecting, cleaning out H.Q. Quarters Chateau	

Cecil

121/5802.

June 1915

Summoned but not copied 121/5802

3rd Cavalry Division

No 121 Sanitary Section 8th Cavalry Division

Vol VI

Ans

Army Form C. 2118.

WAR DIARY
or
INTELLIGENCE SUMMARY.
(Erase heading not required.)

Instructions regarding War Diaries and Intelligence Summaries are contained in F.S. Regs., Part II and the Staff Manual respectively. Title pages will be prepared in manuscript.

SANITARY SECTION — THIRD CAVALRY DIVN.

Hour, Date, Place	Summary of Events and Information	Remarks and references to Appendices
June 1st 1915 Flametinghe	Party digging Latrines & Refuse Pits, and Cleaning up Gen. H.Q. Chateau.	
Ypres	2 Men attached to 17th Fd. Ambs disinfecting at Ramparts, and advanced dressing Station.	
Cambayne Hogebranck 2-6-1915	Party disinfecting (Steam) Huts and Supervision of Bath.	
Ypres Flamertinghe Hogebranck Cambayne	Party disinfecting at the dressing Station. Inspection of Cambayne Grounds & Baths. Party Steam disinfecting Life Cie. dugouts	

WAR DIARY
or
INTELLIGENCE SUMMARY.
(Erase heading not required.)

Army Form C. 2118.

Hour, Date, Place	Summary of Events and Information	Remarks and references to Appendices
3-6-1915 Vlamertinghe	Inspection & cleaning up of Company Grounds	
Hope Hazebrouck	Party working at the dressing Station Baths	
4-6-1915 Vlamertinghe Reserve Hazebrouck	Cleaning up Billets, changed at Camp: Et's Disinfect Motor Ambulance Baths, Supervision of	
5-6-1915 Vlamertinghe	Cleaning officers billet, Pack up ready to move.	
6-6-1915 Hazebrouck	Left Vlamertinghe for Reserve.	

WAR DIARY
or
INTELLIGENCE SUMMARY.
(Erase heading not required.)

Army Form C. 2118.

Hour, Date, Place	Summary of Events and Information	Remarks and references to Appendices
7-6-1915. Renescure	General Routine.	
Hogenacker	Disinfect Ambulance	
8-6-1915. Hogenacker	Baths. Party at Campagne disinfecting Baths. Disinfection at Brobelon	
9-6-1915. Renescure	Disinfection at Campagne. Disinfect Ambulances. Baths Hogenacker.	
10-6-1915. Boesinghem Campagne Renescure	Sanitary Squad with 6th Cav. Fd. Amb. Disinfection 1st Life Guards. Inspection of Gen. H.Q. also Billets	
11-6-1915. Boesinghem Renescure	Party disinfecting Billets at 6 Cav. Fd. Amb. General Routine.	CWW

WAR DIARY
or
INTELLIGENCE SUMMARY.
(Erase heading not required.)

Army Form C. 2118.

Hour, Date, Place	Summary of Events and Information	Remarks and references to Appendices
12-6-1915. Renescure Empayne Hazebrouck	Inspection of Billets. Party Steam Disinfecting.	
13-6-1915 Steenbecque Renescure	Baths and disinfection at Echelon. Party left for disinfection with the North Somersets.	
14-6-1915 Wittes Steenbecque Hazebrouck	Inspection of Billets & Disinfect Huts. Digging Refuse pits at Renescure. Disinfect Billets, Renescure. Steam disinfection Wijes. Baths & disinfection at B. Echelon.	
15-6-1915. Renescure Steenbecque	Water Looking for O.C. Mot. Ambn Div. Steam disinfection Wijes. Baths & disinfection.	CQMS

WAR DIARY
or
INTELLIGENCE SUMMARY.
(Erase heading not required.)

Army Form C. 2118.

Instructions regarding War Diaries and Intelligence Summaries are contained in F.S. Regs., Part II and the Staff Manual respectively. Title pages will be prepared in manuscript.

Hour, Date, Place	Summary of Events and Information	Remarks and references to Appendices
16-6-1915. Renescure Staenbecque Hazebrouck	Inspection of Headquarter Billets. Disinfection. N. Sipos Baths.	
17-6-1915. Staenbecque	General Routine at Renescure Disinfection N. Sipos	
18-6-1915. Hazebrouck	Inspection by Commander-in-Chief at Vandecques Baths.	
19-6-1915. Hazebrouck	Repairing Disinfector Baths.	
20-6-1915.	Water testing for 6 M.V.S. of 6n Div.	
21-6-1915. Blaringhem Staenbecque	N.C.O. party Cleaning at disinfecting Ditches. Inspection re first case of Diphtheria	
Vandecques	Party Steam Disinfecting 2nd Lf Guards	

WAR DIARY
or
INTELLIGENCE SUMMARY.
(Erase heading not required.)

Army Form C. 2118.

SANITARY SECTION
THIRD CAVALRY DIV.

Instructions regarding War Diaries and Intelligence Summaries are contained in F.S. Regs., Part II and the Staff Manual respectively. Title pages will be prepared in manuscript.

Hour, Date, Place	Summary of Events and Information	Remarks and references to Appendices
22-6-1915. Wanrecque Hazebrouck	Sanity Cleaning Ditches at Blaringhem. Steam Disinfecting 3rd Life Guards. Baths.	
23-6-1915. Wanrecque Renescure	Building improvements at H.Q. Stables. Steam Disinfection. Cleaning up Railway, Inspection of Billet. Baths. Hazebrouck.	
24-6-1915. Wanrecque Hazebrouck	Cleaning up Railway, Renescure. Disinfection at 2nd Life Guards.	
25-6-1915. Renescure Hazebrouck	Disinfection. General Routine. Baths & disinfection.	
26-6-1915. Wanrecque	Pack up & Move to new Billet. Steam Disinfection.	
27-6-1915. Renescure	General Routine. Inspection of Billet.	

WAR DIARY
or
INTELLIGENCE SUMMARY.
(Erase heading not required.)

Army Form C. 2118.

Instructions regarding War Diaries and Intelligence Summaries are contained in F.S. Regs., Part II. and the Staff Manual respectively. Title pages will be prepared in manuscript.

Hour, Date, Place	Summary of Events and Information	Remarks and references to Appendices
28-6-1915 Reninghe	Cleaning out Ditches at Reninghe. Inspection of Billets; disinfect Ambulance.	
29-6-1915 Hagebrouck Reninghe	Party left for disinfection at B. Echelon Baths. General Routine.	CRW
30-6-1915. Reninghe Hagebrouck	Inspection of Billets. Steam Disinfection, B. Echelon, and Supervision of Baths.	

3rd Cavalry Division

121/6341

121/6341

Summarised but not copied

12th Sanitary Section

Vol VII

July 1/15

S/

July 1/15

Ans

Army Form C. 2118.

12th Sany: Sectn

WAR DIARY
INTELLIGENCE SUMMARY.
(Erase heading not required.)

Instructions regarding War Diaries and Intelligence Summaries are contained in F.S. Regs., Part II and the Staff Manual respectively. Title pages will be prepared in manuscript.

Hour, Date, Place	Summary of Events and Information	Remarks and references to Appendices
1915 July 1 Reuville Hazebrouck	General Routine Disinfection at B Echelon Hospital (Gas &c Ants) Baths.	
" 2 Reuville "	General Routine Hazebrouck Disinfection at Hazebrouck Baths.	Nil
" 3 Nurdreques "	Construction of Latrine, Urinals & Refuse Pit. urine pit &c for demonstration to 7 & 8 Bns Troops by teams.	Nil
" Bouchevesne "	Disinfecting B Echelon Hospital Baths	Nil
" 4 Reuville	General Routine.	Nil
" 5 Boeseghem	Construction of Latrine, Incinerator, Refuse Pit, urine pit &c for demonstration by 2nd and 10th Gds Brigade.	Nil
" Reuville	1 N.C.O. & 4 men attached to 6th Cavalry Brigade for supervision of all sanitary arrangements.	Nil
" Hazebrouck	Disinfection at Hazebrouck B Echelon Hospl Baths	

(73989) W 4141—463. 400,000. 9/14. H.&J.,Ltd. Forms/C. 2118/10.

WAR DIARY
or
INTELLIGENCE SUMMARY.
(Erase heading not required.)

Army Form C. 2118.

Instructions regarding War Diaries and Intelligence Summaries are contained in F.S. Regs., Part II. and the Staff Manual respectively. Title pages will be prepared in manuscript.

Hour, Date, Place	Summary of Events and Information	Remarks and references to Appendices
1915 July 6th Roussseure	Cleaning yard at A.D.M.S. Bill's Inspection of	nil
" "	Narcoeques cleaning & disinfecting. Returned for 1 K 6 an Field Ambulance	nil
" 7 Roussseure	Bill's Inspection of	nil
" Hazebrouck	Disinfecting at 13 Echelon C.S. Ambulance	nil
" 8 Roussseure	General Routine.	nil
" "	Bill's Inspection of	nil
" "	13 Echelon Hospital	nil
" Hazebrouck	Disinfecting at Hospital 13 Echelon.	nil
" 9 Roussseure	Cleaning Yard A.D.M.S.	nil
" Hazebrouck	Disinfecting 13 Echelon Hospital	nil
" 10 Roussseure	Inspection of Bivouacs of 2nd Field Squadron R.E. and 13 Echelon Ammunition Column.	nil
" "	Instructions sanitary orderly of 2nd Field Squadron in the employment of a sewage filter.	nil
" 11	General Routine	nil

Army Form C. 2118.

WAR DIARY
INTELLIGENCE SUMMARY.
(Erase heading not required.)

Instructions regarding War Diaries and Intelligence Summaries are contained in F.S. Regs., Part II and the Staff Manual respectively. Title pages will be prepared in manuscript.

Hour, Date, Place	Summary of Events and Information	Remarks and references to Appendices
1915		
July 12 Busseaure	Constructing Incinerators for 3rd Field Squadron R.E.	
" "	Inspection of Bivouacs re HQrs IV Bgde RHA & ammunition column	
" "	Clearing ditch rear of camp	
" "	Making troughs for latrines	
" "	Supervising construction of same re latrines, HQrs RHA IV Bgde	
" 13	Constructing incinerator, Amm Column, R.H.A.	
" "	Bivouac inspection of	
" "	Party (1 NCO & 9 men) carrying out sanitary arrangements & recup. of trench digging party of division	
" 14	ditto	
" 15 Neuvillette	Digging latrines &c at new billet, general repairs	
" " Lailly	Party carrying out sanitary arrangements of camp & latrines of trench digging party.	

WAR DIARY
or
INTELLIGENCE SUMMARY.
(Erase heading not required.)

Army Form C. 2118.

Instructions regarding War Diaries and Intelligence Summaries are contained in F. S. Regs., Part II and the Staff Manual respectively. Title pages will be prepared in manuscript.

Hour, Date, Place		Summary of Events and Information	Remarks and references to Appendices
1915			
July 16	Hennington	Bn coming up Yard at British P.O.	
		Bn inspecting 6 looks at 4pm A & other places	CMM
		Rigging Bathing at Billet of Ambulance Drivers also	CMM
		Signal Office (Report Centre)	CMM
		Construction of Incinerator at B.P.O.	CMM
	Pîtom	Inspection of Billets	CMM
		Mining Signal Office re code of messages (Ontario)	
	Grand Caro	Inspection of Chateau (Erneuil Billet)	
	Hennington	Rigging Latrines & refuse pit at billet	
	Scailly	Sanitary Signal attending to Sanitation of Hennington	
		Worked of mini-rigging party	
July 17	Serens	Worked Blanket to 10th Hussars	
	Hennington	Completion of construction of Incinerator at P.O.	
	Pîtom	Inspecting Signal Office after use of Health, also	CMM
		Close at Generals billet, Chateau, Hot Baits.	
	Hennington	Billets Inspection of	
	Soilly	Sanitary Sgt attending to Sanitation, rigging Party	
	18 Lereil	Inspecting Blankets - 10th Hussars	
	" Pîtom	Inspecting Bivouacs of 81 Coy. A.S.C. Signal Section, HQrs	CMM
		R.H.A. (Brigade)	

Army Form C. 2118.

WAR DIARY
or
INTELLIGENCE SUMMARY.
(Erase heading not required.)

Instructions regarding War Diaries and Intelligence Summaries are contained in F.S. Regs., Part II and the Staff Manual respectively. Title pages will be prepared in manuscript.

Hour, Date, Place		Summary of Events and Information	Remarks and references to Appendices
1915 July 19	Hennington Circus	Inspection of Billets. Disinfecting, 10th Hussars.	CMM
" 20	"	"	
" "	Hennington	Inspection of maness of R.H.A. O.C's mess & RHA amm Column	
" "	"	Rigging latrines at farm occupied by Blue horses.	
" "	"	Inspection of Billets	
" 21	"	Disinfecting yard relabel ASm SHOP Billets	CMM
" "	Dicrohel	Inspection of Bivouac area re 3rd Field 85th R.E.	CMM
" "	Locere	Disinfecting, 10th Hussars	CMM
" 22	Hennington	Disinfecting latrines at billet	
" "	Locere	Disinfecting, 10th Hussars	
" 23	Hennington	Disinfecting 2 motor ambulances from B. Echelon Hospital after conveyance of typhoid cases.	CMM
" "	Locere	Disinfecting — 10th Hussars	
" "	Elvertinghe Belgium	Sanitary squad (1NCO & 4 men) with friend skynig Army attending to sanitation at Camp.	CMM

WAR DIARY
or
INTELLIGENCE SUMMARY.
(Erase heading not required.)

Army Form C. 2118.

Instructions regarding War Diaries and Intelligence Summaries are contained in F.S. Regs., Part II and the Staff Manual respectively. Title pages will be prepared in manuscript.

Hour, Date, Place		Summary of Events and Information	Remarks and references to Appendices
1915 July 24	Lovens	Motor Lorry from 3rd Cav Supply Column transferred, also Lorries left i/c of Driver in Stock.	
	Mousbecque	Inspected drains & pit at Chateau, instructions given for abatement of nuisance & digging of grease trap garbage pit.	
	Heuvinghem Grand Bois	Inspection of wells, shoeing clouts. Grounds of Château 61 Cav A.S.C., R.A.A., H.Q.rs	
		" Bivouac site of 3rd Sqnd. 5th R.E.	
	Lovens	20 m perfoming Reveille 9c — 10 th Hussars.	
	Elverdinghe	Sounding Signal with Digging Party marching to Pionisation of Camp.	ours
25 "	"	ditto	ours
" "	Lovens	20 m perfoming, 10 Th Hussars	ours
26 "	"	ditto	
" "	Heuvinghem	Inspection of billets, Heuvinghem	
" "	Elverdinghe	Sounding Action (portion of) with digging Party	
27 "	Lovens	20 m perfoming Reveille, 10 th Hussars	
" "	Elverdinghe	Sounding Action (portion of) with Trench digging Party	ours
28 "	"	ditto	ours
" "	Heuvinghem	Divine Service	ours

Army Form C. 2118.

WAR DIARY
or
INTELLIGENCE SUMMARY.
(Erase heading not required.)

Instructions regarding War Diaries and Intelligence Summaries are contained in F.S. Regs., Part II and the Staff Manual respectively. Title pages will be prepared in manuscript.

Hour, Date, Place	Summary of Events and Information	Remarks and references to Appendices
1915 July 29 Elverdinghe	Sanitary Section (portion of) with trench digging party attached to Squadron of Camp.	
Henninghen	General Routine	
30 Boeseghem	Disinfecting Members, 3rd Dragoon Guards	
Elverdinghe	Sanitary Section (portion of) with trench digging party	
Henninghem	General Routine	
31 Boeseghem	Disinfecting Members, 2nd Dragoon Guards.	
Elverdinghe	Sanitary Section (portion of) with trench digging party	
Henninghem	General Routine.	

August 1915

S/

3rd Garhwal Rifles

13/
6550

Summarised but not copied

12th Aug: letter
Not recd

From 1st to 31st Aug. 1915

August 1915

Army Form C. 2118.

WAR DIARY
or
INTELLIGENCE SUMMARY.
(Erase heading not required.)

Instructions regarding War Diaries and Intelligence Summaries are contained in F.S. Regs., Part II. and the Staff Manual respectively. Title pages will be prepared in manuscript.

Date	Hour Place	Summary of Events and Information	Remarks and references to Appendices
1915			
Aug 1st	HEURINGHEM	General Routine	
	ELVERDINGHE	General Sanitation of Camps of Trench Digging Party	
	BOESEGHEM	Disinfecting Party with 3rd Dragoon Guards	
Aug 2nd	HEURINGHEM	General Routine	
	ELVERDINGHE	General Sanitation of Camps of Trench Digging Party	
	BOESEGHEM	Disinfecting Party with 3rd Dragoon Guards	
Aug 3rd	HEURINGHEM	General Routine	
	ELVERDINGHE	General Sanitation of Camps of Trench Digging Party	
	BOESEGHEM	Disinfecting Party with 3rd Dragoon Guards	
Aug 4th	HEURINGHEM	General Routine.	
	ELVERDINGHE	General Sanitation of Camps of Trench Digging Party	
	THÉROUANNE	WATER TESTING (5 tests) for two Corps	
		Bivouac reconny up & preparing billets for Cavalry Corps	
Aug 5th	HEURINGHEM	General Routine.	
	ELVERDINGHE	General Sanitation of Camps	
	THEROUANNE	Preparing billets for Cavalry Corps.	
Aug 6th	HEURINGHEM TO RADINGHEM	MOVE - General Routine & preparing own Camp etc	Cav.

Army Form C. 2118.

WAR DIARY
or
INTELLIGENCE SUMMARY.
(Erase heading not required).

Instructions regarding War Diaries and Intelligence Summaries are contained in F. S. Regs., Part II and the Staff Manual respectively. Title pages will be prepared in manuscript.

DATE	PLACE	Summary of Events and Information	Remarks and references to Appendices
Aug 7th	RADINGHEM	Repairing pump, laying on water to Chateau (Hospital) for B. Echelon & F.A.E. Digging latrines, urine pits, 2 Greasetraps, Garbage pits, refuse pits	
	WANDONNE	Rigging latrines &c at HQrs Chateau	
	LINGHEM	Disinfecting party with 3rd Dragoon Guards.	
Aug 8th	RADINGHEM	Plumbing at Chateau (B. Echelon Hospital) Garbage Routine.	
	WANDONNE	Latrines Routines H.Q.rs	
	LINGHEM	Disinfecting party with 3rd Dragoon Guards.	
Aug 9th	RADINGHEM	Plumbing at Chateau (B Echelon Hospital) Inspection of Chateau Grounds.	
	ARQUES	Disinfecting Room occupied by case of Cerebro-Spinal fever previous to arrival of 3rd tous-ius Supply Column.	
	FAUQUEMBERQUES	Inspection of Divisional HQ Billets.	
	LINGHEM	Disinfecting Party with 3rd Dragoon Guards.	
Aug 10th	RADINGHEM	Repairing of Orghead, building them and/or for Hospital.	
	FAUQUEMBERQUES	Inspection of Divisional HQ billets/where Billets	
	DENNEBROUCQ	Disinfecting Billets of 3rd Signal Squadron R.E.s	
	FLECHINELLE COLLIERY	Inspection of Baths at Colliery	
	HERVARRE	Case of Vacuum needles	CMM

(7.5989) W4141—463. 400,000. 9/14. H.&J.Ltd. Forms/C. 2118/10.

WAR DIARY
or
INTELLIGENCE SUMMARY.

(Erase heading not required.)

Army Form C. 2118.

Instructions regarding War Diaries and Intelligence Summaries are contained in F.S. Regs., Part II and the Staff Manual respectively. Title pages will be prepared in manuscript.

Date	Hour	Place	Summary of Events and Information	Remarks and references to Appendices
1915				
Aug 11th		RADINGHEM	Planning at Hotshop. Completion of General Purpose Small Arm Workshop unit. Erase map for Armourers & Small Arms workshop unit. Also tracings for same unit.	
		DENNEBROUSQ	Inspecting Republican Billets. Supervising working party clearing out ditch opposite 3rd Dragoon Guards.	
		LINGHEM	Disinfecting party with 3rd Dragoon Guards HQrs	
		FAUQUEMBERGUES	Inspection of Billets previous and HQrs	
Aug 12th		RADINGHEM	General Routine.	
		LINGHEM	Disinfecting party with 3rd Dragoon Guards.	
		FAUQUEMBERGUES	Inspecting Billets in Hgne.	
Aug 13th		RADINGHEM	General Routine. Making enlarged scale map of area of Division for Inspection of Horse spotting. Inspection of Divisional Ambulance Billets.	
		FAUQUEMBERGUES		
		LINGHEM	Disinfecting party with 3rd Dragoon Guards.	
Aug 14th		RADINGHEM	General Routine. — Making enlarged scale map of Area of Division for 2nd div. spotting.	
		LINGHEM	Disinfecting Party with 3rd Dragoon Guards.	
		FAUQUEMBRGS	Inspecting Billets Divisional H.Qrs	
Aug 15th		RADINGHEM	General Routine	
		FAUQUEMBRGS	ditto	
		LINGHEM	Disinfecting Party with 3rd Dragoon Guards.	

WAR DIARY
or
INTELLIGENCE SUMMARY.

(Erase heading not required.)

Army Form C. 2118.

Instructions regarding War Diaries and Intelligence Summaries are contained in F.S. Regs., Part II and the Staff Manual respectively. Title pages will be prepared in manuscript.

DATE	PLACE	Summary of Events and Information	Remarks and references to Appendices
Aug 16	RADINGHEM	General Routine. Drawing area of ground for trf. I.O.S. Sporting.	
	FAUQUEMBERGUES LINGHEM	Inspection of billets of personnel. Visit to Disinfecting Party with 3rd Surgeon Generals.	
Aug 17	RADINGHEM	Surveying hospital area for purpose of a plan. General Routine.	
	FAUQUEMBERGUES LINGHEM	Inspection of billets. Disinfecting Party with 3rd Surgeon Generals.	
Aug 18	RADINGHEM	Surveying hospital grounds & making plan of same. General Routine.	
	FAUQUEMBERGUES LINGHEM	Inspection of Billets (including burial places at D.A.D.O.S.) Disinfecting Party with 3rd Surgeon Gls.	
Aug 19	RADINGHEM	Drawing ground plan of Hospital Grounds & Chateau. Completing typing of new idea for Orl.I.O.S. Sporting. General Routine.	
	FAUQUEMBERGUES WANDONNE COYECQUE RADINGHEM	Inspection of billets. 3rd Field Squadron (General Sanitation) 1st Life Guards ditto Surveying ground plan of Hospital Gds & Chateau General Routine	
Aug 20	FAUQUEMBERGUES	Inspecting Sanitary arrangements of 16th & 87th Sur. Gd. Ambs. Inspection of Billets.	Cecil

WAR DIARY
or
INTELLIGENCE SUMMARY.
(Erase heading not required.)

Army Form C. 2118.

Date	Hour, Date, Place PLACE	Summary of Events and Information	Remarks and references to Appendices
1915 Aug 21	RADINGHEM ESTREE BLANCHE FRUGES FAUQUEMBERGUES	General Routine. Disinfecting party under North Somerset yeomanry. Inspection of Tents by Sanitary Officers (2 min overhaul Engr R. Hylds) Inspection of Billets	
Aug 22	RADINGHEM ESTREE BLANCHE FRUGES FAUQUEMBERGUES	General Routine – making another trug of area. Disinfecting party with N.S.yeo. Men detailed for sanitary inspection of camps. Notices (R.H.Hylds) Inspection of Billets	
Aug 23	RADINGHEM ESTREE BLANCHE FRUGES FAUQUEMBERGUES	General Routine. Disinfecting Party with N.S. Yeo. Inspection of Camps R.H.Gold. Inspection of Billets.	
Aug 24	RADINGHEM ESTREE BLANCHE FRUGES FAUQUEMBERGUES	General Routine. Disinfecting Party with N.S. Yeo. Inspection of R.Hylds Camps. Inspection of Billets	
Aug 25	RADINGHEM FRUGES ESTREE BLANCHE COYECQUE WANDONNE FAUQUEMBERGUES	General Routine. Inspection of Camps & R.Hylds. Disinfecting party with N.S. Yeo. Visit to lot Life Brigade re case of Enteric. "3rd Field Squadron" R.E. re suspected case of infectious disease. Inspection of Billets	

WAR DIARY
or
INTELLIGENCE SUMMARY.

(Erase heading not required.)

Army Form C. 2118.

Instructions regarding War Diaries and Intelligence Summaries are contained in F.S. Regs., Part II and the Staff Manual respectively. Title pages will be prepared in manuscript.

Date	Hour, Date, Place PLACE	Summary of Events and Information	Remarks and references to Appendices
Aug 26	RADINGHEM	General Routine.	
	FRUGES	Inspection of Billets & Recruits	
	NEDON	Disinfection of parts, with 1st Royal Dragoons	
	HAZEBROUCK	Lorry Journey to fetch Bivy. sheets for Recruits	
	FAUQUEMBERGUES	Inspection of Billets	
Aug 27	RADINGHEM	General Routine.	
	FRUGES	Inspection of Billets R.H.Gds.	
	NEDON	Disinfecting party with 1st Royal Dragoons.	
	FAUQUEMBERGUES	Inspection of Billets	
Aug 28	RADINGHEM	General Routine.	
	FRUGES	Inspection of Billets & Recruits	
	NEDON	Disinfecting Party with 1st Royal Dragoons	
		Visit re suspected case of pneumonia measles at 7th Cav Bgde	
Aug 29	FAUQUEMBERGUES	Inspection of Billets	
	RADINGHEM	General Routine.	
	FRUGES	Inspection of camps & Billets Recruits.	
	FAUQUEMBERGUES	Inspection of Billets.	
	NEDON	Disinfecting Party with 1st Royal Dragoons.	

(signature)

Army Form C. 2118.

WAR DIARY
or
INTELLIGENCE SUMMARY.
(Erase heading not required.)

Instructions regarding War Diaries and Intelligence Summaries are contained in F.S. Regs., Part II. and the Staff Manual respectively. Title pages will be prepared in manuscript.

Date	Hour. Date. Place PLACE	Summary of Events and Information	Remarks and references to Appendices
1915			
30 Aug	RADINGHEM	Constructing large improvised grease trap storage pit (to accommodate dump + along line) for B Echelon C.F.A.	
		General Routine.	
	FRUGES	Inspection of Officers Rifles	
	NEDON	Transferring Party work 1st Royal Dragoons	
	FAUQUEMBERGUES	Inspection of Billets.	
Aug 31	RADINGHEM	Completion of grease trap storage pit.	
		General Routine	
	NEDON	Disinfecting Billets + work for Royal Dragoons.	
	FAUQUEMBERGUES	Inspection of Billets.	
			CAM

Appendix No 3. "Out of Bounds" Notice.

CONTAGIOUS DISEASE

PROHIBITED TO TROOPS

BY ORDER

Date Of Infection

3rd Cavalry Division

Summaried but not acted

12th Sans hay letter

S/
Sept 1915

121/
6920

Col IX
Sept. 15

WAR DIARY
or
INTELLIGENCE SUMMARY
(Erase heading not required.)

Army Form C. 2118

Instructions regarding War Diaries and Intelligence Summaries are contained in F.S. Regs., Part II. and the Staff Manual respectively. Title Pages will be prepared in manuscript.

Place	Date	Hour	Summary of Events and Information	Remarks and references to Appendices
Rudingham	1/9/15	—	General routine	
Neclon	"	—	Disinfecting 1st Royal Dragoons	
Bucquemaque	"	—	Inspection of Billets etc	
Fringes	"	—	ditto. A.Q.G. Northampton Cpl.	
Rudingham	2/9/15	—	General Routine A.R.T.	
Neclon	"	—	Disinfecting party with 1st Royal Dragoons	
Bucquemaque	"	—	Inspection of Billets etc	
Fringes	"	—	ditto A.C.T.	
Rudingham	3/9/15	—	General Routine	
Neclon	"	—	Disinfecting 1st Royal Dragoons	
Bucquemaque	"	—	Inspection of Billets	A.C.C.T.
Fringes	"	—	ditto	
Rudingham	4/9/15	—	General Routine	
Waidburne	"	—	Disinfecting ditch near C.O.C. Chateau	
Neclon	"	—	Disinfecting 1st Royal Dragoons	
Bucquemaque	"	—	Inspecting Billets Personnel N.9 + S.	A.C.C.T.
Fringes	"	—	" Royal Horse Guards	A.C.C.T.
Rudingham	5/9/15	—	General Routine	
Neclon	"	—	Disinfecting 1st Royal Dragoons	
Bucquemaque	"	—	Inspection of billets Div. H.Q.N. R.H.Amb	
Fringes	"	—	"	A.C.C.T.

Army Form C. 2118

WAR DIARY
or
INTELLIGENCE SUMMARY

(Erase heading not required.)

Instructions regarding War Diaries and Intelligence Summaries are contained in F.S. Regs., Part II. and the Staff Manual respectively. Title Pages will be prepared in manuscript.

Place	Date	Hour	Summary of Events and Information	Remarks and references to Appendices
Rollingham	6/9/15	—	General Routine	
Hedon	"	—	Disinfecting 1st Royal Dragoons.	
Fauquembergues	"	—	Inspection of Billets &c	
Bruges	"	—	" " " A.T.	
Rollingham	7/9/15	—	General Routine	
Hedon	"	—	Disinfecting 1st Royal Dragoons. (Shrub (horse drawn) Curtain Steam	
Bruges	"	—	Inspection of Billets &c (Disinfector)	
Fauquembergues	"	—	" " " A.T.	
Rollingham	8/9/15	—	Disinfecting blankets 13 Echelon C.F.A.S. Hospital. (Portable hose disinfector)	
Everville }	"	—	Inspecting Sanitary arrangements of Labour Battalion 61R	
Velles }				
Begum }	"	—	Disinfecting blankets &c (men's shirts, trousers, & shoe apparel) H.Q.rs.	
Follard }				
Fauquembergues	"	—	Inspecting billets & camps Divisional Headquarters,	
Bruges	"	—	" " camps, R.H. Gds. A.T.	
Rollingham	9/9/15	—	General Routine — Disinfecting blankets 13 Echelon Hospital (Bozo	
Everville }	"	—	Instructing newly formed Sanitary Squad of 6th Labour Battalion on (Disinfector)	
Velles }			Digging latrines, Urine pits, Refuse Dumps &c &c.	
Begum }	"	—	Disinfecting blankets &c 6th Escot Brigade H.Q.rs.	
Follard }				
Fauquembergues }	"	—	Inspection of Billets &c A.T.	
Bruges }				

WAR DIARY or INTELLIGENCE SUMMARY

Army Form C. 2118

Instructions regarding War Diaries and Intelligence Summaries are contained in F.S. Regs., Part II. and the Staff Manual respectively. Title Pages will be prepared in manuscript.

(Erase heading not required.)

Place	Date	Hour	Summary of Events and Information	Remarks and references to Appendices
Rudinghem	10/9/15	—	General Routine. - Disinfecting Blankets, B Echelon Hospital.	
Zudor Pitfour	"	—	Disinfecting Blankets & Kits HQrs 6th Cavalry Brigade.	
Fauquembergues	"	—	Inspecting Billets Rapids Divisional Headquarters	A.T.
Rudinghem	11/9/15	—	Disinfecting Blankets &c B Echelons Hospital	
Zepuis Pitfour	"	—	Disinfecting Blankets &c HQrs 6th Cav Brigade.	
Fauquembergues	"	—	Inspection of Billets 9C	A.T.
Rudinghem	12/9/15	—	General Routine.	
Zepuis Pitfour	"	—	Disinfecting Kits & men of Signallers HQrs 6th Cav Bgde & Blankets of Southerly Section.	
Fauquembergues	"	—	Inspecting Billets.	A.T.
Rudinghem	13/9/15	—	Converting 4 gallon petrol cans into latrine bucket seats in lieu of shallow trench latrine on account shortage of ground space. General Routine.	
Zebrin Pitfour	"	—	Disinfecting party with HQrs 6th Cavalry Brigade.	
Zuigo Fauquembergues	"	—	Inspecting billets, camps 9C	A.T.

Army Form C. 2118

WAR DIARY
or
INTELLIGENCE SUMMARY

(Erase heading not required.)

Instructions regarding War Diaries and Intelligence Summaries are contained in F. S. Regs., Part II. and the Staff Manual respectively. Title Pages will be prepared in manuscript.

Place	Date	Hour	Summary of Events and Information	Remarks and references to Appendices
Radinghem	14/9/15	—	Converting 4 gallon petrol cans into latrine buckets	
"	"	—	Disinfecting blankets 13 Echelon Hospital	
Illies	"	—	Disinfecting blankets &c (o.k.) Cavalry Field Ambulance.	
Bruges	"	—	} Inspecting Billets &c A.T.	
Fauquembergues	"	—		
Radinghem	15/9/15	—	Disinfecting blankets 13 Echelon Hospital.	
"	"	—	General Routine	
Illies	"	—	Disinfecting (o.k.) C.F.A.	
Bruges	"	—	} Inspecting Billets &c R.Officers & Other Head Qrs. A.T.	
Fauquembergues	"	—		
Radinghem	16/9/15	—	General Routine (including Sanitary Police duty) Sanitary Section	
"	"	—	Lorry journey to Le Notre Sur Bois for firewood for Sanitary Section	
"	"	—	13 Echelon.	
Wardrecques	"	—	Disinfecting Officers' closet, filling in latrines &c	
Bruges	"	—	} Inspection of Billets. A.T.	
Fauquembergues	"	—		
Radinghem	17/9/15	—	Constructing latrines.	
"	"	—	Lorry journey (18 miles) fetching local for 13 Echelon Hospital.	
Fauquembergues	"	—	} Inspection of Billets A.T.	
Bruges	"	—		
Radinghem	18/9/15	—	Constructing latrines	
"	"	—	Inspecting billets &c of 13 Coy 10th Labour Battalion.	
"	"	—	Lorry journey fetching bricks for incinerator	
Illies	"	—	Disinfecting blankets &c "C" Battery R.H.A.	
Bruges	"	—	} Inspection of Billets. A.T.	
Fauquembergues	"	—		

WAR DIARY or INTELLIGENCE SUMMARY

(Erase heading not required.)

Army Form C. 2118

Instructions regarding War Diaries and Intelligence Summaries are contained in F. S. Regs, Part II. and the Staff Manual respectively. Title Pages will be prepared in manuscript.

Place	Date	Hour	Summary of Events and Information	Remarks and references to Appendices
Radinghem	19/7/15	—	On burying & digging latrines "B" Echelon &c. Repairing incinerators for "B" Echelon & F.As. & Field Ambulances Workshop unit & building a further one for Horse Transport Section B.F.As.	
Nordausques	" "		Lorry journey to Steehun conveying blankets for disinfection.	
Tingues	" "			
Tatingchem	" "		At G.O.C. Chateau — digging latrines &c.	
Radinghem	20/7/15		Inspecting billets R.H.A &ds & Divisional Head Quarters. A.T.	
" "	" "		Constructing fresh incinerator pits (pits 2ft deep — 2ft square — & gals petrol cans (punched from inside) let in the earth about 6ins) Well pits to be filled in as fast as possible for the purpose. A.T.	
" "	" "		Completion of incinerator for Horse Transport Section C.F.As.	
Steehun	" "		Disinfection of blankets & sleeping suits for B. Echelon Hospital	
" "	" "		Lorry journey to Steehun. A.T.	
Tingues	" "			
Tatingchem	" "		Inspection of Camps & Billets.	
Radinghem	21/7/15		Lorry journey to Steehun (5 am.) for disinfecting, returning early, but equipment, shoes & disinfector left in the care of the Maire of Steehun.	
" "	" "		Lorry journey to Tanqueberque to fetch 2 men attached to div. H.Qr. A.T.	
Westrehem	" "		MOVE from Radinghem to Westrehem. A.T.	
(Sercus) (Thienouwe)	22/7/15		Digging latrines at Camp	
" "	" "		Lorry journey to Radinghem for firewood, & to No More au Bois for firewood.	
" "	" "		Digging officers' latrines, mens' latrines & building incinerator.	
" "	" "		Collecting firewood & preventing pollution. A.T.	
Westrehem	23/7/15		Digging further latrines while pits also another Incinerators.	
" "	" "		Collecting firewood for prevention of pollution. A.T.	
Westrehem	24/7/15		MOVE from Westrehem to Labuissière (beyond Bruay) starting by. A.T. standing by. A.T.	
Labuissière	25/7/15		Standing by — General Routine. Digging latrines. A.T.	
do	26/7/15		Starting by — 7pm received instruction to proceed immediately to R.N.C.D. near AIRE, departed from Labuissière 8-15 pm. A.T.	

WAR DIARY
or
INTELLIGENCE SUMMARY
(Erase heading not required.)

Army Form C. 2118

Place	Date	Hour	Summary of Events and Information	Remarks and references to Appendices
Rinxy	27/9/15	—	Digging latrines, lines &c. for own unit. Inspecting Camp of 8th Brigade B Echelon. Fatigue used by O/C R.E. for conveying Reinforcements &c. A.T.	
"	28/9/15		Inspecting Camp of A/gr, A.S.C. & B Echelon O.S. A.9c 8th Brigade. A.T.	
"	29/9/15		N.C.O. Supervising general cleaning up of Camp of 8th Brigade. A.T. General Routine. — do —	
"	30/9/15		— Building incinerator, grease trap soakages pits &c. A.T.	

12/7341

3rd Military Division

Enumerated but not copied

12th Sanitary Section
Pol X
Oct 15

Oct 16
5/5

WAR DIARY
or
INTELLIGENCE SUMMARY
(Erase heading not required.)

Army Form C. 2118

Instructions regarding War Diaries and Intelligence Summaries are contained in F.S. Regs., Part II. and the Staff Manual respectively. Title Pages will be prepared in manuscript.

Place	Date	Hour	Summary of Events and Information	Remarks and references to Appendices
	1915 Octr			
RINCQ	1		General Routine	A.L.T.
"	2		Inspection of Camps, horse lines &c of HQrs & B Echelons	
"	3		Inspecting Barn for A. Qrs 3rd Cav. Divn. Inspecting Camps of B Echelons	
"	4		General Routine.	A.L.T.
"	5		ditto	
"	6		ditto	
"	7		ditto	A.L.T.
FERFAY	8		Officer - inspecting & diagnosing case of measles amongst Airlines.	
LAUTHY a la(W) AUCHELLE (2)			General Inspection of "B" Battery R.H.A. also (2)1st Royal Dragoons	
RINCQ	9		General Routine	
FERFAY			General inspection of North Somerset Yeomanry	
RINCQ	10		General routine.	A.L.T.
REINBERT			General inspection of 3rd Dragoon Guards. Arranging punks at mines for 6th & 8th Brigades.	
RINCQ	11		General Routine	
HURIONBALLE			Inspection of Essex Yeomanry	
RINCQ	12		General routine. Inspection of "G" Battery R.H.A. & Ammunition Column.	
BURBURE				
RINCQ	13		General Routine. Inspection of Divisional Supply Column.	A.L.T.
LILLERS				

WAR DIARY
or
INTELLIGENCE SUMMARY
(Erase heading not required.)

Army Form C. 2118

Instructions regarding War Diaries and Intelligence Summaries are contained in F. S. Regs., Part II. and the Staff Manual respectively. Title Pages will be prepared in manuscript.

Place	Date 1915	Hour	Summary of Events and Information	Remarks and references to Appendices
RINCQ	OCTR. 14		General routine	
LIERES	"		Inspection of Royal Horse Guards	
BOURECQ	"		" billets &c of Divisional Headquarters & R.H.A. Amn: Column.	M.I.T.
RINCQ	15		"	
ECQUEDECQUES	"		Inspecting sanitary arrangements of 10th R. Hussars.	M.I.T.
RINCQ	16		General Routine	
REINBERT	"		Sanitary inspection of 3rd Dragoon Guards.	
RINCQ	17		General routine	
FERFAY	"	MORN	Sanitary inspection of N. S. Yeomanry	
HURIONVILLE	"	A'NOON	" " " Essex Yeo:	
FERFAY	"		Disinfection (THRESH) of blankets belonging to 13 Echdm. C.F.As. 9 H.Q. & 6 CAV. BDE	M.I.T.
RINCQ	18		General routine	M.I.T.
AUCHELLE	"		Sanitary inspection of 1st Royal Dragoons.	M.I.T.
REINBERT	"		" " " 3rd Dragoon Gds.	
BURBURE	"		" " " "G" Battery R.H.A.	
RINCQ to FRUGES	19		MOVE.	
FRUGES	20		Billeting	
do	21		Building incinerator at rear of Field Amb: Workshop unit. General Routine.	M.I.T.
do	22		One Corporal & 3 men detached & attached for temporary duty to 1st Life Guards, 42nd Leinster Yeomanry & "K" Battery R.H.A. Digging latrines for own unit & making scoops for general use at latrines.	

WAR DIARY
or
INTELLIGENCE SUMMARY
(Erase heading not required.)

Army Form C. 2118

Place	Date	Hour	Summary of Events and Information	Remarks and references to Appendices
FRUGES LAIRES	1915 Oct 23		General routine. Inspected "G" Battery R.H.A.	M.I.T.
FRUGES	" 24		Making or borrowing 4 gall. petrol cans into latrine buckets.	
do	" 25		One man ordered & sample attached to H.Qrs. 8th Brigade for executive Sanitary work. Inspected Auxiliary Horse Transport Company.	M.I.T.
CAPELLE SUR LA LYS	"		Disinfected (Thresh disinfector) Barns + billets of Essex Yeomanry.	
"	"		do (Thresh disinfector) Blankets & kits of Essex Yeo: Arranged disinfection of kits + men bathed, & teams of horses sprayed with formalin + H.C.I. mixture while men bathing.	M.I.T.
FLECHINELLE	"		Arranged trucks for formalin (50 spray tanks or mines)	
FRUGES	" 26		General Routine.	M.I.T.
CAPELLE SUR LA LYS	"		Stables of Essex Yeomanry disinfected by spray formalin disinfection also at Relinghem.	
"	"		Disinfecting (Thresh) blankets & kits of men of Essex Yeomanry.	
FRUGES	" 27		Inspecting H.Q. & A.S.C. & of 3rd Cavalry Details, also 3rd Signal Troop.	
VINCLY	"		Disinfecting with Spray formalin for births, trucks for stables, Essex Yeomanry (with Thresh) blankets & kits of men of Essex Yeomanry.	
NATTRINCHEM	" 28		Disinfecting blankets & kits of Essex Yeomanry.	
"	"		Spray disinfection of billets & barns &c.	
ENQUIN LES MINES	"		Arranging for disinfection of 10th Hussars.	M.I.T.

WAR DIARY
or
INTELLIGENCE SUMMARY
(Erase heading not required.)

Army Form C. 2118

Instructions regarding War Diaries and Intelligence Summaries are contained in F.S. Regs., Part II. and the Staff Manual respectively. Title Pages will be prepared in manuscript.

Place	Date 1915	Hour	Summary of Events and Information	Remarks and references to Appendices
LUIGY HEZECQUES	Sept 28		Inspection of 3rd Signal Squadron " Ammunition Column R.H.A.	M.J.T.
LIGNY LES AIRES	"		Advising re disposal of refuse 1st Royal Dragoons.	
FRUGES	29		General routine.	
MATTRINGHEM	"		Re-inspecting billets of Marks of Essex Yeomanry (Squad) (Troop 2) thanks to c/o of men of Essex Yeomanry.	M.J.T.
BEAUMETZ LES AIRES	30		Inspected 14th mobile veterinary Section	M.J.T.
FLECHIN	"		" " Royal Horse Guards.	
MATTRINGHEM	"		Disinfection of Marks of billets; also blankets &c/c of men of Essex Yeo.	
"	31		" " " "	
	OCTR		There are at present 15 N.C.Os men attached for temporary duty c/o Jullens 1 man to each Brigade HQrs for executive work & 2 Cpls & 10 Acting L/Cpls attached to the 9 Regiments & 3 Batteries for administrative sanitary work. Each man will submit a monthly report of his work to the Head Qrs of the Section & included in this Diary.	M.J.T.

No 12 Sanitary Sec.
3rd Cav. Div.

Nov 1
V or XI

12/7671

Summarised but not copied

Nov 1915
S/
12/7671

WAR DIARY
or
INTELLIGENCE SUMMARY
(Erase heading not required.)

Army Form C. 2118.

Place	Date 1915	Hour	Summary of Events and Information	Remarks and references to Appendices
Bruges Mathringhem	Nov 1 "		Inspecting Leicester Yeomanry at Couzelle hielle & Denty. Disinfecting clothing at Essex Yeomanry	
Bruges Rumilly	2 "		General Routine. Inspected 1st Life Guards.	M.I.T.
Bruges Londonecky Harmans	3 "		General Routine. Inspected 2nd Dragoon Guards.	
Armentes	"		" North Somerset Yeomanry.	
Bruges	4		30 H.g. all petrol cans taken over to "E" Batty R.H.A. for use as troops urinals at billets. Also how to use a latrine & shelters at Divisional Rest Station.	M.I.T.
Mathringhem	"		Inspected "E" Battery R.H.A.	
Bruges	5		" Essex Yeomanry. Inspected billets, stables, &c., of H.Q. 3rd Cav. Bgd. Assisting to erect latrine, &c., shelters at D.R. Station.	
Lignyers also	"		Inspected 1st Royal Dragoons	
Bruges	6 "		Disinfecting Divisional Rest Station (Thrush). Constructing Grease trap &c at D. Rest Station.	M.I.T.
"	7 "			
"	8 "		Inspected HQrs 3rd Cav. Div. Billets &c. General Routine	

WAR DIARY or INTELLIGENCE SUMMARY

Army Form C. 2118

Instructions regarding War Diaries and Intelligence Summaries are contained in F. S. Regs., Part II. and the Staff Manual respectively. Title Pages will be prepared in manuscript.

(Erase heading not required.)

SANITARY SECTION
No. ......
Date. Nov 1915
THIRD CAVALRY DIV.

Place	Date	Hour	Summary of Events and Information	Remarks and references to Appendices
Fruges Caudescour	Nov 9		General routine. Disinfecting huts & disposal of refuse.	
Fruges	10		General routine.	
Hesdinville	11		Superintending bathing & disinfecting at Colline (Vermycelli & N.C.I. powder used to sprinkle on seams of trousers for crushing, men's clothing disinfected well they were bathing).	M.O.I.
Bruges	12		General Routine.	
"	"		" "	
Hesdinville	13		Superintending bathing & disinfecting at Colline (same procedure).	
" "	"		" " " "	
Fruges	14		General routine. Testing Thresh Disinfector after being repaired. It appeared in good working order.	M.O.I.
"	"		Drawing up Bow Disinfector at Divisional Rest Station. Endeavouring to arrange baths in the Brigade Area.	
"	15		Disinfecting at Divisional Rest Station. Endeavouring to obtain thoroughly portable baths at B.R.C.S. for used in various huts of Divisional Area.	A.C.I.
Fruges	16		Disinfecting at Rest Station, and spraying out milk vessel, as stated to be used for "B" Echelon horses.	
"	17		General routine.	

WAR DIARY
or
INTELLIGENCE SUMMARY
(Erase heading not required.)

Army Form C. 2118

Instructions regarding War Diaries and Intelligence Summaries are contained in F. S. Regs., Part II. and the Staff Manual respectively. Title Pages will be prepared in manuscript.

SANITARY SECTION
No. ...
Date Nov 1915
THIRD CAVALRY DIV.

Place	Date 1915	Hour	Summary of Events and Information	Remarks and references to Appendices
Sturges	Nov 18		Thrush, disinfecting at Divisional Rest Station. Inspecting Ammunition Column & Auxe Horse Transport Coy A.S.C.	
"	19		Thrush, disinfecting at Divisional Rest Station.	M.W.T.
"	20		Inspection Divisional Headquarters billets.	
Oresquy	"		General routine.	
Sturges	21		Inspecting 1st Royal Dragoons.	
Hesmonds	"		General routine.	
Sturges	22		Inspecting billets of Auxe Horse Transport Coy, A.S.C.	
"	23		Suspected case of measles. Inspecting billets of Ammunition Column.	
Huqueliers	"		General routine. Thrush, disinfecting at 7th Brigade H.Qrs. (disinfecting Dungaree Suits, blankets &c of men returned from Trench digging).	M.W.T.
"	"		Arranging Baths for 7th Brigade, & inspected disinfecting.	
"	24		Thrush, disinfecting at 7th Brigade H.Qrs.	
Pernois Embry	"		Inspected villages for cases of Infectious Disease & discovered several cases of measles amongst civilians.	
Hesmonds	"			
Sturges	"		General routine. (50-Gall petrol cans returned in lorry to 1st Life Gds. for use as latrine pails.)	M.W.T.

WAR DIARY or INTELLIGENCE SUMMARY

Army Form C. 2118

SANITARY SECTION
No. NOV
Date 1915
THIRD CAVALRY DIV.

Place	Date 1915	Hour	Summary of Events and Information	Remarks and references to Appendices
Bruges	Novr 25		Lorry journey to Meauconville Farm & out for Disinfector (& inspection of lorry)	
Houquelien	" 26		Thrush, disinfecting at 4th Brigade H.Qrs.	
Bruges	" 27		General routine	
Offin	" 28		Thrush, disinfecting at 3rd Dragoon Guards	
"	"		" "	
Bruges	" 29		General routine	
"	"		Thrush, disinfecting at "B" Echelon Isolation Hospital (Scabies)	M.C.T.
Offin	"		" " 3rd Dragoon Guards.	
Bruges	" 30		" " "B" Echelon Isolation Hospital.	
"	"		Spraying gutters & drains of patients with formalin.	
Offin	"		Thrush, disinfecting at 3rd Dragoon Guards. (while under clothes & disinfected trousers issued with hot irons)	
			Routine work of N.C.Os men on detached duty with Headquarters, Regiments & Batteries of the Division :-	
	NOVR.		Regular inspection of billets, stables, latrines, u.e.g.e, supervising construction of incinerators, digging of latrines, general sanitary convenience. Spraying with disinfectant, billet stables &c, and General sanitary work under direction of M.O. of the various units	M.C.T.

1st Cav. Div.

F/25/11

12th Sanitäry Res.

Ang / Vol XII

Summarised but not copied

Dec 1915
/S/

D.A.A.G., 1.,
G.H.Qrs., 3rd Echelon.

This diary belongs to
No 12 Sanitary Section,
3rd Cavalry Division.
The O.C., is Captain
A.G.G.Thompson, R.A.M.C.
T.F.

G. A. Lawson
Captain & Q'M'
for Lieut.-Colonel
Officer i/c R.A.M.C. Section,
General Hd. Qrs. 3rd Echelon

[Stamp: A.G. OFFICE AT THE BASE — 31 JAN.1916 — R.A.M.C. SECTION]

Vol XII

Confidential

O i/c R.A.M.C. Sect.

Can you please say to what unit the attached War Diary belongs?

F D Bone
for DAAG

29.1.16

A.G.'s OFFICE AT THE BASE
CENTRAL REGISTRY
30 JAN 1916
C.R. No. 140/809.

WAR DIARY
INTELLIGENCE SUMMARY
(Erase heading not required.)

Army Form C. 2118

Instructions regarding War Diaries and Intelligence Summaries are contained in F. S. Regs., Part II. and the Staff Manual respectively. Title Pages will be prepared in manuscript.

Place	Date	Hour	Summary of Events and Information	Remarks and references to Appendices
Bruges (Officer Nieuwville)	1915 Nov 1		Disinfecting with Thresh Disinfector at Seating Hospital.	
"	"		Disinfecting (with formalin & spray) rooms at a farmhouse & civilian hut lately occupied by Belgians 70-10 each. R&S 9c of 3rd Dragoon Guards	
Bruges Ypres	2		Cleaned machine (Turning mat & D'manvel areas for Infectious Disease clothing). Thresh disinfection of R&S 9c of 3rd D.Gs. While tents &c were being disinfected their trousers were either ironed with hot iron or sprayed with disinfectant Grease powder.	
Bruges	3		Thresh disinfection of blankets, R&S, sleeping kits of Seating patients at location Hospital.	
"	"		Arranging baths for Divisional troops.	
"	"		Thresh, Steam disinfection of R&S 9c of 3rd D.G.S. (continued)	
Bruges	4		" " " blankets & Seating patients (contd.)	
Coffin	"		" " " R&S 9c of 3rd D.G.S. continued.	
Bellevue	"		Disinfecting with Spray & formalin Mess room & sleeping Quarters of contacts of man suffering from cerebro-spinal meningitis also orderly room which man slept in. Bedding so brought away in lorry for steam disinfection.	M.U.T.
Bruges	5		Steam Disinfection of bedding of the man from Bellevue. Disinfection of lorry with formalin. Twenty remaining disinfected bedding.	
"	6		Steam disinfection of sleeping kits, R&S 9c of Seating patients at Seating Hospital.	M.U.T.

WAR DIARY
or
INTELLIGENCE SUMMARY
(Erase heading not required.)

Army Form C. 2118

Instructions regarding War Diaries and Intelligence Summaries are contained in F. S. Regs., Part II. and the Staff Manual respectively. Title Pages will be prepared in manuscript.

Place	Date 1916	Hour	Summary of Events and Information	Remarks and references to Appendices
Bruges	7		Going up boiler at house to be used for Divisional Baths	
Rumilly	"		Arranging baths.	
Creguy	"		Finish steam disinfection, 1st Royal Dragoons.	
Bruges	8		General routine.	
	"		Interviewing m.o. 6th Brigade arranging for water carts to be used	
			& latrines to be covered.	McW.
Creguy	"		Finish steam disinfection of R.H.Q. of 1st Royal Dragoons	
Bruges	9		General routine	
Creguy	"		Steam disinfection, 1st Royal Dragoons, continued	
Rumilly	"		Inspecting Sanitary arrangements Stables &c of 1st Life Guards,	
Humbert	"		" " " " " " 10th Hussars.	McT.
Bruges	10		Steam disinfection at Isolation Hospital	
Creguy	"		Disinfector moved.	
Cuilly	"		Inspection of Billets Leicester Yeomanry.	
Nieuwkapelle	"			
Bruges	11		General routine. Inspection of Sanitation of Field Ambulance & Northorpe	
			Unit & Divisional Rest Station	
Creguy	"		Steam Disinfection, 1st Royal Dragoons.	
"	"		Inspection of Sanitation "Div. H.Q."	
Bruges	12		Inspection of H.Q. Billets ("Div. H.Q.")	McT.
Cregny	"		Steam Disinfection at 1st Royal Dragoons (continued).	
Rumilly	"			

WAR DIARY
or
INTELLIGENCE SUMMARY
(Erase heading not required.)

Army Form C. 2118

Instructions regarding War Diaries and Intelligence Summaries are contained in F. S. Regs., Part II. and the Staff Manual respectively. Title Pages will be prepared in manuscript.

Place	Date	Hour	Summary of Events and Information	Remarks and references to Appendices
Bruges	19/5 April 13		Steam disinfection, Scabies Hospital. Letter writing, board "Divisional Baths".	McV.
"	"			
Bregny Suiden	"		Steam disinfection, 1st Royal Dragoons (continued)	
"	"		Inspection of billets of 34 D. & 8th Brigade.	
Bruges	14		General routine	
"	"		Pairing board "Divisional Baths"	
Bregny	"		Steam disinfection, 1st R.H.G. (contd).	
Bruges	15		General routine.	
"	"		Steam Disinfecting. 1st Royal Dragoons (contd).	McV.
Joxy	"		Inspection, Sanitary arrangements, 2nd Dragoon Guards.	
Offin	"			
Bruges	16		Preparing hutto for use following day.	
Joxy	"		Steam disinfection, 1st Royal Dragoons (contd)	
Marcken	"		Inspection of 3 cases of Diphtheria. Examined, placed tub of hutments.	
Bruges	17		Supervising to Divisional Baths.	
Roijon	"		Disinfecting room after case of measles.	
Bruges	"		Steam disinfection, Scabies Hospital.	
Bruges	18		Supervising bathing of Divisional Troops.	
Courtrai & Menin	"		Inspected billets of 3rd Field Squadron	
Bruges	19		General nuisance. Horse placed out of bounds for case of Diphtheria.	McV.
Menomnel	"		Investigating measles case.	

WAR DIARY
or
INTELLIGENCE SUMMARY
(Erase heading not required.)

Army Form C. 2118

Instructions regarding War Diaries and Intelligence Summaries are contained in F.S. Regs., Part II. and the Staff Manual respectively. Title Pages will be prepared in manuscript.

Place	Date 1915	Hour	Summary of Events and Information	Remarks and references to Appendices
Bruges	Decr 20		Visited all Schools in the town for cases of Infectious Disease	Mel
"	"		Supervising Divisional baths.	
Hazemond	"		Steam disinfection, North Somerset Yeomanry.	
Bruges	21		Supervising Divisional baths.	
Hazemond	"		Steam disinfection, N. Somerset Yeo (contd).	
Embury	"		Inspected Sanitary arrangements of Essex Yeomanry.	
Bruges	22		Supervising Divisional baths.	
"	"		Steam disinfection Scabies Hospital	
Leburg	"		" N.S. Yeo. (contd).	
Marant	"		Inspected farm & noted cases of foot + mouth disease existed, and two who removed therefrom and prohibited the sale or otherwise of milk	
Loffin	"		Discovered case of measles notified same.	
Bruges	23		Supervising Divisional baths.	
"	24		" " "	
Marant	"		Steam disinfection Scabies Hospital	
"	"		" " Royal Horse Guards. (Equipment, Arms & Clothing of contacts of Spot. mouth disease)	
Bruges	25			
"	26			

General Routine

Army Form C. 2118

WAR DIARY
or
INTELLIGENCE SUMMARY
(Erase heading not required.)

Instructions regarding War Diaries and Intelligence Summaries are contained in F.S. Regs., Part II. and the Staff Manual respectively. Title Pages will be prepared in manuscript.

Place	Date	Hour	Summary of Events and Information	Remarks and references to Appendices
	1915			
Bruges	Dec 27		Supervising Divisional Baths.	
"	28		" " "	M.S.
			Steam disinfection, Scabies Hospital.	
			Inspection, 10th Hussars.	
Lempry	29		Supervising Divisional Baths.	
Bruges			Investigation (case of diphtheria, trooper in North Somerset Yeomanry	
Litraer			Inspection, Billets of North Somerset Yeomanry	
Hazard				
Bruges	30		Supervising Divisional Baths.	
			Steam disinfection, Scabies Hospital.	M.S.
			" Essex Yeomanry.	
St Vincent			Investigation (case of typhoid in 3rd Dragoon Guards)	
Ottir				
Bruges	31		Supervising Divisional Baths.	
Lamont	"		Steam Disinfection, Essex Yeomanry (contd).	
1st to 31st			The Sanitary Section was attached to Regimento Batteries & Aux H.T. Coys continued to	
Dec 1915			carry out their work. The majority of supervision & superintending of general	
			sanitation. In the majority of cases where spraying and available, pipelime	
			spraying of stables, billets & mens rooms with disinfectant. In some places	
			it has been possible to fit shelters & provide to gate of cesspits by other	
			similar methods for latrine accommodation. Similar water supply are	
			disinfected given water-borne sanitary at common ways according to	
			methods at hand. Some of turf or bricks, others of two filled tank earth	M.S.

M.W. Thompson Capt.

3rd Cav. Bde. Sanitary Sec.
(No 72 Sany Section Sam 1912
vol. I?

Jan 1916.?

Christmas Message from His Majesty The King.

The following message has been received :—

"Another Christmas finds all the resources of the Empire still engaged in War, and I desire to convey on my own behalf, and on behalf of the Queen, a heartfelt Christmas greeting and our good wishes for the New Year to all who, on Sea and Land, are upholding the honour of the British name. In the officers and men of my Navy, on whom the security of the Empire depends, I repose, in common with all my subjects, a trust that is absolute. On the officers and men of my Armies, whether now in France, in the East, or in other fields, I rely with an equal faith, confident that their devotion, their valour and their self-sacrifice will, under God's guidance, lead to Victory and an honourable Peace. There are many of their comrades now, alas, in hospital and to these brave fellows, also, I desire, with the Queen, to express our deep gratitude and our earnest prayers for their recovery.

Officers and men of the Navy and Army, another year is drawing to a close, as it began, in toil, bloodshed and suffering; but, I rejoice to know that the goal to which you are striving draws nearer into sight.

MAY GOD BLESS YOU AND ALL YOUR UNDERTAKINGS."

GEORGE, R.I.

The following reply has been despatched :—

To :—HIS MAJESTY THE KING,
Buckingham Palace,
London.

The Army in France under my Command desires to be allowed to express its warmest thanks to Your Majesty and to Her Majesty the Queen for the gracious message received. On behalf of the troops I respectfully beg Your Majesties to accept the most heartfelt good wishes of all ranks for Xmas and the New Year and an expression of their firm and lasting determination to prove themselves worthy of the great trust which Your Majesty reposes in us.

From :—SIR DOUGLAS HAIG.

Christmas Day, 1915.

1st Printing Co., R.E. G.H.Q. 2000

Special Order of the Day.

By Field-Marshal SIR J. D. P. FRENCH, G.C.B., O.M., G.C.V.O., K.C.M.G., Commander-in-Chief, British Army in the Field.

In relinquishing the command of the British Army in France I wish to express to the officers, non-commissioned officers and men, with whom I have been so closely associated during the last sixteen months, my heartfelt sorrow in parting with them before the campaign, in which we have been so long engaged together, has been brought to a victorious conclusion.

I have however, the firmest conviction that such a glorious ending to their splendid and heroic efforts is not far distant, and I shall watch their progress towards this final goal with intense interest, but in the most confident hope.

The success so far attained has been due to the indomitable spirit, dogged tenacity which knows no defeat, and the heroic courage so abundantly displayed by the rank and file of the splendid Army which it will ever remain the pride and glory of my life to have commanded during over sixteen months of incessant fighting.

Regulars and Territorials, Old Army and New Army have ever shown these magnificent qualities in equal degree.

From my heart I thank them all.

At this sad moment of parting my heart goes out to those who have received life-long injury from wounds, and I think with sorrow of that great and glorious host of my beloved comrades who have made the greatest sacrifice of all by laying down their lives for their country.

In saying good-bye to the British Army in France I ask them once again to accept this expression of my deepest gratitude and heartfelt devotion towards them, and my earnest good wishes for the glorious future which I feel to be assured.

Field-Marshal,
Commanding-in-Chief, the British Army in France.

18th December, 1915.

Army Form C. 2118.

WAR DIARY
or
INTELLIGENCE SUMMARY.
(Erase heading not required.)

Instructions regarding War Diaries and Intelligence Summaries are contained in F.S. Regs., Part II and the Staff Manual respectively. Title pages will be prepared in manuscript.

Hour, Date, Place	Summary of Events and Information	Remarks and references to Appendices
Bruges JAN 27th	Drafty man at Henty (Lei Yeo) suspect Enteric Divisional Baths.	M.L.T.
Sailly Lab. "		
Noyelles "	Routine.	
Bruges 28th	Drift to billets at farm of M. Desgraviliers (Campbell Newman) occupied by 3rd Field Squadron R.E.	
Sailly "		
Noyelles "	Began eating mud from the roads.	M.L.T.
Noyelles 29th	Routine.	
Sailly 3 30th	Inspected billets etc.	
Sailly 31st	Built pit incinerators and a number of urine pits.	M.L.T.

(SANITARY SECTION THIRD CAVALRY DIV.)

WAR DIARY
or
INTELLIGENCE SUMMARY

(Erase heading not required.)

Army Form C. 2118

Instructions regarding War Diaries and Intelligence Summaries are contained in F. S. Regs., Part II. and the Staff Manual respectively. Title Pages will be prepared in manuscript.

Place	Date	Hour	Summary of Events and Information	Remarks and references to Appendices
Frugès Sailly Labourse	JAN 23rd		Disinfecting after case of measles at LEBIEZ N.S. Yeomanry Completing erection of ablution benches	MJT
Frugès Sailly Noyelles	24th " "		Drifting billets etc of measles case at N.S. Yeo. Inspection of billets Constructing pathways around huts. Had whole camp (1 Troop) removed to civil hospital, Rittrue. Disinfected hutment	
Sailly	25th "		ditto Completing latrines, digging urine pits and constructing incinerators near public latrines	
Frugès "	26th "		Party proceeded to Aire-en-bercant (Royal Horse Guards) for drifty billets etc. Inspecting billets at Henly (Leicester Yeo.) Suspected case of Enteric. Supervision of Divisional Baths. Removal of suspected infection case to Hospital from Coupelle Neuve (3rd Field Squadron R.E.)	MJT
Sailly Labourse	"		Constructing two incinerators in compound of recreation room	MJT
Noyelles	"		Began construction of portable latrine shelters. Routine	

WAR DIARY
or
INTELLIGENCE SUMMARY
(Erase heading not required.)

Army Form C. 2118

Instructions regarding War Diaries and Intelligence Summaries are contained in F. S. Regs., Part II. and the Staff Manual respectively. Title Pages will be prepared in manuscript.

Place	Date	Hour	Summary of Events and Information	Remarks and references to Appendices
Sailly Labourse	JAN 16th		Digging latrines and urine pits	
"	17th		Constructing Incinerator, burning refuse, constructing Special latrines for Officers and the G.O.C. at Chateau	M.J.S.
Noyelles Fringes	18th		Construction of latrines and offices. Partly staining at, Disinfected barn at Hely (Scarlet Fever case)	
Sailly Labourse	"		Cleaning courtyard etc. at G.O.C. chateau	M.J.S.
Noyelles Fringes	19th		Routine Disfg. Blankets &c. with Thresh at Scabies Hospl.	
Noyelles	"		General supervision of sanitary work	
Sailly Labourse	"		Constructing urine pit	
"	20th		Constructing 4 urine pits, 1 latrine, 1 incinerator Supervised civilians from of Latrine found. House patroling made. Pump ordered.	
Noyelles	21st		Inspecting, clearing refuse	
Noyelles	"		Constructing pathways made of slag around the huts	M.J.S.
Sailly Labourse	22nd		Digging latrines for 15th Hussars, refixing ablution benches for Machine Gun drivers.	
Noyelles	"		Constructing pathways.	

WAR DIARY
or
INTELLIGENCE SUMMARY
(Erase heading not required.)

Army Form C. 2118

Instructions regarding War Diaries and Intelligence Summaries are contained in F. S. Regs., Part II. and the Staff Manual respectively. Title Pages will be prepared in manuscript.

Place	Date	Hour	Summary of Events and Information	Remarks and references to Appendices
Noyelles	JAN. 10th		Digging urine pits in rear of huts. Baths commenced with system of changing underclothing at bath.	M.S.
Verquigneul Noyelles	11th		Adopted a cart for entrenching barrow. Fatigue parties cleaning up camp, installing more urine pits, and refuse pits.	
Fruges	12th		Steam disinfection at Essex Yeo. finished and party returned to unit.	
" Noyelles	12th		Party disinfecting at Scabies Hospital Reconstruction of latrines at camp, filling in old latrines which had become a nuisance, and went insanitary.	M.S.
"	13th		Baths. 4 incinerators built. Routine.	
"	14th		" 2 Incinerators built. Routine.	
"	15th		" Digging latrines, making ablution benches and general supervision of fatigue parties on sanitary work	

SANITARY SECTION
No.
date.
THIRD CAVALRY DIV.

WAR DIARY
or
INTELLIGENCE SUMMARY
(Erase heading not required.)

Army Form C. 2118

Instructions regarding War Diaries and Intelligence Summaries are contained in F. S. Regs., Part II. and the Staff Manual respectively. Title Pages will be prepared in manuscript.

Place	Date 1916	Hour	Summary of Events and Information	Remarks and references to Appendices
Fruges	Jan. 1st		General Routine Supervising Divisional Baths, etc.	
"	2nd		ditto	
Mesnires	"		Sub. taken from tents. Inspected diphtheritic curtains	
St. Denoeux	3rd		Steam Disinfection at Essex Yeo. (cont'd)	
Maisoncelle: Nuncq	"		Sub. taken from tents. Inspected diphtheritic curtains	
Prinques	"		General Routine. Sanitary etc.	
Capelle Marck	4th		Inspected billets of 3rd Field Squadron R.E.	
Fruges	5th			
Hesmond	"		Inspected billets etc. of Notts Scouant Yeomanry.	
Fruges	6th	1-15 pm	Officer and men proceed in motor lorry to join Dismounted Division.	M.T.
Verquingneul	"		Arrive and take up quarters.	
"	7th		Officers' inspection of the area allotted to the Section. Divisional Baths & General Sanitation	
Fruges	"		Officer & men proceeded by motor lorry to Noyelles.	M.T.
Verquingneul	8th		Digging large refuse pits at back of huts and billets. Diphtheria pre. civilian men & soldier men. Obtained fatigue men & cleared camp of litter and refuse.	
Noyelles	"	9th	burying same in the pits	
"	"			
Fruges	"		Disinfecting billet and blankets of Sgt. Goldsworthy, Essex Yeo. (case of mabeles)	

3rd Cavl Bge

12th Lancers Section

Feb. 1916.

No 12 Sany Section
Sanitary Section
3 Cav Div
Feb
Vol XIII

No 12 Sany Section

Army Form C. 2118.

WAR DIARY
or
INTELLIGENCE SUMMARY.
(Erase heading not required.)

Instructions regarding War Diaries and Intelligence Summaries are contained in F. S. Regs., Part II and the Staff Manual respectively. Title pages will be prepared in manuscript.

Hour, Date, Place		Summary of Events and Information	Remarks and references to Appendices
1916 Feby 1	Fruges Noyelles	Superintending Divisional Baths & disinfecting. Bathing of parties, boiling of troops coat. Care of men in sch Batt. developed in the trenches.	A.T.
" 2	Fruges Noyelles	Superintending Divisional Baths. Inspection of Divisional Headquarters. Men detailed for sanitary duty with R.H.A. Brigade at Auxi[?]. Went on with Public Cat's Washpits [?] the week.	A.T.
" 3	Fruges Noyelles	Superintending Divisional Baths. Inspecting latrines A.S.C. & disinfecting. Three portable latrine shelters put up. Disinfecting continued. Drainage of road cleaned and repaired.	
" 4	Fruges Noyelles Sailly	Superintending Divisional Baths. Same work continued. Disinfected horse pen & con[?] wagons.	A.T.
" 5	Fruges Noyelles Sailly	General routine. Routine continued. Latrine shelter put up.	

Army Form C. 2118.

WAR DIARY
or
INTELLIGENCE SUMMARY.
(Erase heading not required.)

Instructions regarding War Diaries and Intelligence Summaries are contained in F.S. Regs., Part II and the Staff Manual respectively. Title pages will be prepared in manuscript.

Hour, Date, Place	Summary of Events and Information	Remarks and references to Appendices
1916 Feby 6 Fruges Sailly Noyelles	General routine. Path to latrine put up yesterday made today. Built two incinerators.	
" 7 Fruges Annezin Sailly Noyelles	Superintending Divisional Baths. Dumpated room for works. Disinfected loft for nurses. Coated mud from Roads. Made paths round to huts.	
" 8 Fruges Lotinhe Noyelles	Superintending Divisional Baths. Examined pitting from a destroyed chateau and arranged for drainage. Rebuilt an incinerator. Mud removal & clay paths cont.	
" 9 Fruges Noyelles	Superintending Divisional Baths. Construction of Latrine shelters cont. mud cartd & paths cont.	
" 10 Fruges Noyelles	Superintending Divisional Baths. Completed Latrine shelter. Routine cont.	
" 11 Fruges Noyelles Sailly	Superintending Divisional Baths. Went round with O/C Sanitary Section 1st Division. Routine work cont.	

WAR DIARY
or
INTELLIGENCE SUMMARY.

(Erase heading not required.)

Army Form C. 2118.

Instructions regarding War Diaries and Intelligence Summaries are contained in F.S. Regs., Part II and the Staff Manual respectively. Title pages will be prepared in manuscript.

Hour, Date, Place		Summary of Events and Information	Remarks and references to Appendices
1916			
Feby 12	Fruges Norelles	General routine. Burnt rubbish. Routine cont.	AT
Feby 13	Fruges Norelles	General routine. Routine cont.	
14	Fruges Aire for Lilers Norelles	Superintending tents. Burks. Spraying billet at "6" Squadron Essex 960 & disinfecting 14 blankets from above billet in Fruges. Continued clearing up. Handed over to incoming division.	
15	Fruges Hesmond Sailly	Reinsurance Ducks. Spraying billet of "A" Sqdn N°5 Gho (Mumps) N° 5 Ward D.R.S. for whoop'cass. Cleared up rubbish the alleby abroad it.	W.
16	Fruges.	Reinsurance Burks. Spraying Ward at D.R.S. Visit of Verquigneul to Fruges.	

WAR DIARY
or
INTELLIGENCE SUMMARY.
(Erase heading not required.)

Army Form C. 2118.

Instructions regarding War Diaries and Intelligence Summaries are contained in F.S. Regs., Part II. and the Staff Manual respectively. Title pages will be prepared in manuscript.

Hour, Date, Place		Summary of Events and Information	Remarks and references to Appendices
1916 Feby 17	Surges	Divisional Baths. Thordisinfector broke down and Huapelin.	
18	Surges Boulzero	Divisional Baths. Spraying billets of 4 cases of Measles at Essex yeo	AT
19	Surges	Issuing two disinfectors as Soames Ward	
20	Surges	Elemental mushie	
21	Surges Boulzero	Divisional Baths. - Spraying two billets in "C" Squadron area (Boulzero) after evacuation of measles (Essex yeo.)	AT
22	Surges	Divisional Baths.	

WAR DIARY or INTELLIGENCE SUMMARY

Army Form C. 2118

Place	Date	Hour	Summary of Events and Information	Remarks and references to Appendices
Fungo Moulero	1916 23/2		Divisional Baths. Spraying huts after evacuation of 3 cases of measles Essex Yeo "E" Squadron	
Fungo Moulero	24/2		Divisional Baths. Spraying billets after evacuation of measles cases Essex Yeo.	N.T.
Fungo	25/2		Divisional Baths.	
"	26/2		ditto.	
"	27/2		General routine	
"	28/2		Divisional Baths	
Embarr	29/2		ditto. Arrangements for dealing with measles epidemic amongst Essex Yeo. modified.	
	19/2 to 29/2		The N.C.Os recalled from Regiments to forward with Section to Verquigneul rejoined their Regiments on the 18th Feby & recommenced duties on the 19th Feby in connection with the Supervision of the Sanitary work, Such as Emptying incinerators, inspection of billets, latrines &c &c.	N.T.

No. 12 Sanitary Section.

March 1916.

3 C

12 Sanitary Sec
Vol XIV

No. 12 Section 2nd London
Sanitary Section, Army C.F.S.

WAR DIARY
or
INTELLIGENCE SUMMARY
(Erase heading not required.)

Army Form C. 2118

SANITARY SECTION
Date MAR 1916
THIRD CAVALRY DIV.

Place	Date	Hour	Summary of Events and Information	Remarks and references to Appendices
1916 March	1st		Divisional Headquarters, 3rd Cavalry Division - Frugés.	
Hesmond	1		Disinfecting with Spray & Formalin a Loft room in Estaminet used as a Mess & Storehouse, and blankets of men sleeping near to as case of Mumps.	
Fruges Herly	"		Bathing 56 men at our Baths. Suspected case of measles examined. Leicester Yeo.	
Aubin	2		Spraying with formalin after evacuation of five cases, the following:- One of Mumps. Bedding & blankets of patients & contacts. Straw being burnt & room containing these beds & cavales, Sprayed with Formalin	[initial]
Herly	"		1 room containing 4 cavales. Sprayed with Formalin	
Hesmond	"		2 cases of Mumps:- 2 bedrooms & 1 outhouse, bed, bedding & underclothing	
Fruges Aubin	"		Sprayed & Formalin Bathing 8 of men at our Div. Baths	
Fruges	3		Spraying with Formalin after evacuation of Infectious Diseases. (3 measles 1 mumps) 1 Room at an Estaminet with 2 window bed & bedding - Hay loft at Farmyard	
Hesmond			2 cavales (wet clothing & linear burnt) - Bedroom & two hay rooms & beds & bedding Sprayed - Stable & mess room, bedding & bed of invalid clothing	
Aubin Fruges	"		Bathing 42 men at our Divisional Baths	
Embry Herly			Inspector of violation measures taken by Essex Yeo.	
			Leicester Yeo.	[initial]

WAR DIARY or INTELLIGENCE SUMMARY

Army Form C. 2118

(Erase heading not required.)

Instructions regarding War Diaries and Intelligence Summaries are contained in F. S. Regs., Part II. and the Staff Manual respectively. Title Pages will be prepared in manuscript.

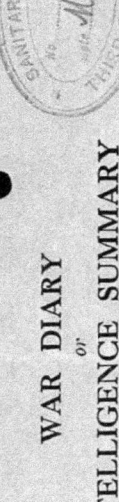

SANITARY SECTION MAR 1916 THIRD CAVALRY DIV.

Place	Date	Hour	Summary of Events and Information	Remarks and references to Appendices
Helmond Cavalry Barracks	1916 Mar 4		Spraying after evacuation of 3 cases of Infectious Jaundice (1 Mumps 2 Mumps). Barn left 3 blankets 4 towercoat – Another barn – tops at Jevers 2 H blankets 9 overcoat 9 horse rug sprayed formalin.	A.
Bourlers St Denoeus Lombry	5		Sprayed with formalin four worn's bed & bedding 35 articles of clothing 9 towercoat. After evacuation of three cases of infectious disease. Examined suspected cases in Esser Luister Yeomany.	
Helmond Cavalry Barracks Hamond	6		After evacuation of five cases of Infectious Disease 3 rooms 1 Kay loft 9 several blankets 9 articles of clothing sprayed with formalin. Bathing 33 men at Divisional Baths. Inspection of latrine rooms of North Somerset Yeo.	
Bourlers Stranges	7		After evacuation of one case of S.D. one Barn 9 7 blankets sprayed with formalin. Straw burnt. Bathing 61 men at Divisional Baths.	A.

1875 Wt. W593/826 1,000,000 4/15 J.B.C. & A. A.D.S.S./Forms/C. 2118.

WAR DIARY or INTELLIGENCE SUMMARY

(Erase heading not required.)

Army Form C. 2118

Instructions regarding War Diaries and Intelligence Summaries are contained in F.S. Regs., Part II. and the Staff Manual respectively. Title Pages will be prepared in manuscript.

Place	Date	Hour	Summary of Events and Information	Remarks and references to Appendices
Zillebeke Pontey Brussels	1916 Mar 8		Four cases of Infectious Disease evacuated, Sieur rooms & one Barn, 15 blankets, bed & bedding sprayed with formalin & straw burnt.	
Bruges Hennuel Eulroy	"		Bathing 52 men at Tori Baths. Inspected suspicious cases in Ess & Lieuten Yeo.	AZ
Bruges Ascomul Hennuel	9		One new room Civilian bed & bedding & 4 blankets sprayed with formalin. Bathing Ergmin at Tori Baths. Examined suspicious civilian & inmates. Arranged for isolation billet for suspects of North Somst Yeo.	
Boulders Zillebeke Pontey Attendres Bruges	10		Disinfecting with spray & formalin after evacuation of sick cases of Inf. Regt. Thurning and farm loft, 35 blankets, civilian beds, bedding & straw burnt.	AZ
	"		Bathing 68 m.en at Divisional Baths. Inspected sanitary arrangements of Anx Horse Transport.	
Bruges Eulroy Scurps	11		Routine. Examined 3 suspicious cases in Ess & Yeomany. Inspected Latrines, billets & Kitchen etc of 10 th Hussars.	AZ

WAR DIARY
or
INTELLIGENCE SUMMARY
(Erase heading not required.)

Army Form C. 2118

Place	Date	Hour	Summary of Events and Information	Remarks and references to Appendices
Bruges	1916 Mar 12		General routine	
Bruges Hoogstade Rousbrugge Eulrry St Ricquiers	13		Divisional baths (64 men bathed) one case of Infectious arrived & sent. Re-disinfected with spray of formalin thrush. Disinfection of blankets, kits etc, Essex yeo. Issue yeo (porkn) – 152 articles. Inspected sanitary arrangements of Essex Yeo.	M
Bruges St Ricard Roesbrugge Hoogstade	14		Divisional baths (92 men bathed) After enquiry of one case of scabies, 1 room at a farm & civilian bed & bedding sprayed with formalin thrush. Disinfection of blankets (88 in number) for Essex yeo. Traced source of Infection (scabies was in bed life spread to Murray from Wes. Yeo. Inspected Sanitation of 7th Brigade H.Q.	M
Bruges Pothure Adinkerke Rousbrugge Henry Aulen Reyon	15		Divisional Baths. (56 men bathed) Disinfection by means of spray of formalin after evacuation of 2 cases of Infections Disease. 1 barn, 1 room at farmhouse, 22 articles (including 16 blankets) civilian bed & bedding. Three L-D inspecting blankets etc of Essex yeo (93 articles) Inspected relation memoria Blues Yeo. Inspected Sanitary arrangements of 8th Brigade H.Q. 6 a	M

WAR DIARY
or
INTELLIGENCE SUMMARY

(Erase heading not required.)

Army Form C. 2118

Instructions regarding War Diaries and Intelligence Summaries are contained in F. S. Regs., Part II. and the Staff Manual respectively. Title Pages will be prepared in manuscript.

Place	Date	Hour	Summary of Events and Information	Remarks and references to Appendices
Truges	1916 May 16		After evacuation of a case of German measles at Point Bel Station, disinfecting one room and first articles of bedding. 10 divisional baths (93 men bathed). Advised changes in Cartier Sanitary Arrangements. Examined inspected rinders in D.R.S. Inspected sanitation of 3rd Field Squadron R.E.	MT
Coupelle Neuve				
Truges Matringhem Coupelle Saints-les- Ennins	17 " "		Divisional Baths (31 man bathed). Owing to outbreak of German measles, busy re-disinfected (spray of formalin) Three disinfection of billets, prior to its use by Yeo (about 60 animals) undergoing from 3rd Bus Boi Boulehead (9 horses) (finished 19.30 am including lot) Inspected sanitation of C Battery R.H.A.	MT
Truges Embry Aire-sur-l...	18 " "		Divisional Baths (cleaning up). Three disinfecting for Essex Yeo. Stables, hito & (about) Boxwelle. Went to Royal Horse Guards re examine inspected care of German measles.	MT
Truges Bouleus Nimboul Wezingham Assinval	19 " "		General routine 3 rooms & 3 cubicles (bedding sprayed with formalin after case of Measles. A case of Infectious enteritis occurred, billets sprayed with formalin at the place Inspected Sanitation of R.H. Wing.	MT

WAR DIARY
or
INTELLIGENCE SUMMARY
(Erase heading not required.)

Army Form C. 2118

Instructions regarding War Diaries and Intelligence Summaries are contained in F. S. Regs., Part II. and the Staff Manual respectively. Title Pages will be prepared in manuscript.

Place	Date	Hour	Summary of Events and Information	Remarks and references to Appendices
Bruges Morlan Wyngnnham Gilly Hin in hut Transent	1916 Mar 20		Divisional Baths. (61 men bathed) Two cases of Spekious disease - billets ye sprayed with formalin. Threats - Disinfecting for Essex Yeo - Blankets Kits ye - about 150 articles Inspected Infusion arrangements in R.H.G. huts. Inspected sanitary arrangements of Divisional Training School.	W.
Bruges Verchocq Ruisseau Alinncham Embry caputte Ville	21		Divisional Baths. (66 men bathed) Disinfecting by means of Spray & formalin a room in the house after one check of typhoid case of contacts isolated. Also one room at a farm 3 blankets 2 pillows & bedding disinfected, spray & form dis. a case of mumps to insect to fever secured the billet ye was disinfected with spray & form dis. Disinfecting (Church) for Essex Yeo - Blankets ye Inspected sanitation of Ammunition Column Inspected . . . C. Battery R.H.A.	W.
Bruges Embry " Ruisseau Bruges Embry Reland Verchocq Crepen	22 23		Divisional Baths. (143 men bathed) one man billet & clothing sprayed with formalin & straw burnt after Disinfecting (Church) Blankets & Kits of Essex Yeo. (40 articles) Inspected articles received ? Essex Yeo. " " " S. A. C. L. E. Ambulance Divisional Baths. (32 men bathed) Fattal pump & septic can pit in O.R.S. Disinfecting (Church) for Essex Yeo - Blankets & Kits (approx 60 articles) Examined pitedocare in Eincah yeo. Inspection of Infection wagons of 1st Life Guards Examined suspected case of mumps was to W. Royal Dragoons.	W.

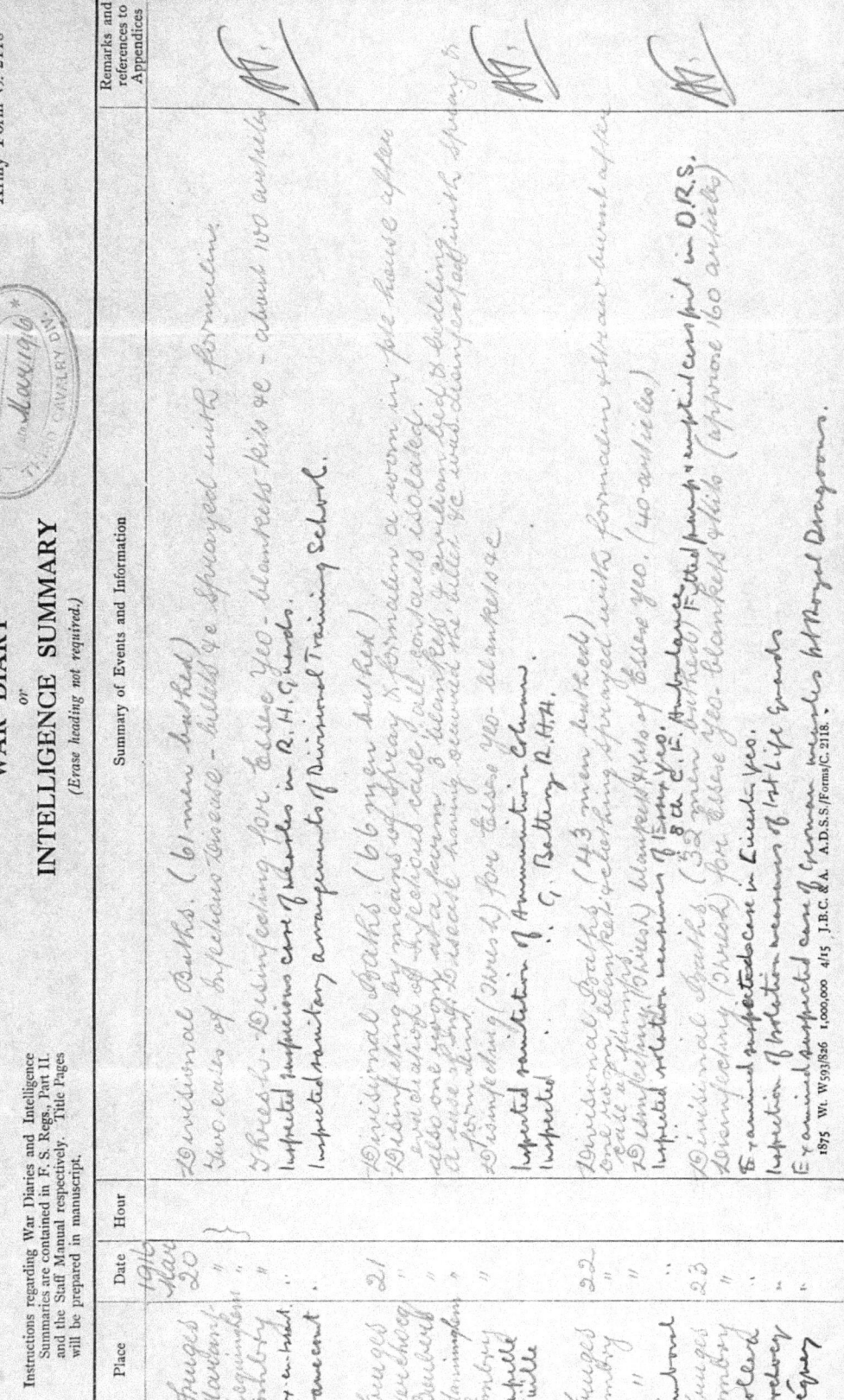

WAR DIARY or INTELLIGENCE SUMMARY

Army Form C. 2118

Instructions regarding War Diaries and Intelligence Summaries are contained in F.S. Regs., Part II. and the Staff Manual respectively. Title Pages will be prepared in manuscript.

(Erase heading not required.)

SANITARY SECTION — Mar 1916 — THIRD CAVALRY DIVN.

Place	Date 1916	Hour	Summary of Events and Information	Remarks and references to Appendices
Bruges Roelers	Mar 24		(1) Urinal baths (20 men buckets). (2) Rooms (one containing 18 men) disinfected by means of spray formalin, also blankets of all the men and four overcoats (No 2 and 5) after disinfection of the rest of the room treated	
Lovegny Bijvoorde	" "		Disinfecting with spray formalin bedroom used by wife & mother of officers ill with cerebro-spinal meningitis. Disinfecting brush doses 720 – blankets (18 rooms)	A.T.
Bruges Verslag Eessenad	" 25 " "		(1) Urinal baths (cleaning baths & establishment) (10 personnel assigned to "B" Battery for use as latrines buckets. Inspection of billets & after removal of Infectious case to by means of Brush Disinfector (12 loads)	
Trouvecourt	"		" Kloove of Issue 70 by means of Brush Disinfector. Inspected sanitation of Divisional Training School.	
Bruges Houthulst	" 26 "		General routine. (1) Disinfecting by means of spray formalin blankets 90 after 1 case of Inf. Disease.	
Rouler Houpelines	" "		Also one small store house where another infectious case had slept. Disinfection of billet 90 after removal of Infectious case.	A.T.
	"		Tried urine inspection (menbu in B/7th Brigade H.Q. & gulling in 7th C.F.A. Brigade infection arrangements.	

WAR DIARY
or
INTELLIGENCE SUMMARY

(Erase heading not required.)

Army Form C. 2118

Instructions regarding War Diaries and Intelligence Summaries are contained in F.S. Regs, Part II. and the Staff Manual respectively. Title Pages will be prepared in manuscript.

SANITARY SECTION
No. ...
Date May 1916
THIRD CAVALRY DIV.

Place	Date	Hour	Summary of Events and Information	Remarks and references to Appendices
Fruges	1916 May 27	..	Divisional Baths. (39 men bathed.) Thresh Disinfector at Seabier Hospital. (8 loads)	M.T.
Boisinville Montreuil	..	..	Endeavoured to trace connection of marks on pump column A.S.C.	
Fruges	28	..	Thresh Disinfector - Seabier Hospital - (7 loads) Divisional Baths. (104 men bathed)	M.T.
Marant	..	..	Inspected intestion arrangements of Machine gun squadron.	
Fruges	29	..	Divisional Baths (51 men bathed) Thresh Disinfection - Seabier Hospital. (5 loads)	M.T.
Francourt	..	..	Machine can in Divisional Training school. Advised intestion biquives.	
Fruges	30	..	Divisional Baths (52 men bathed)	M.T.
Crépy	..	..	Examined suspected Typhoids in 1st Royal Dragoons	
Hesmond	..	..	Arranged disinfection of latrine etc of Leicester Yeo.	

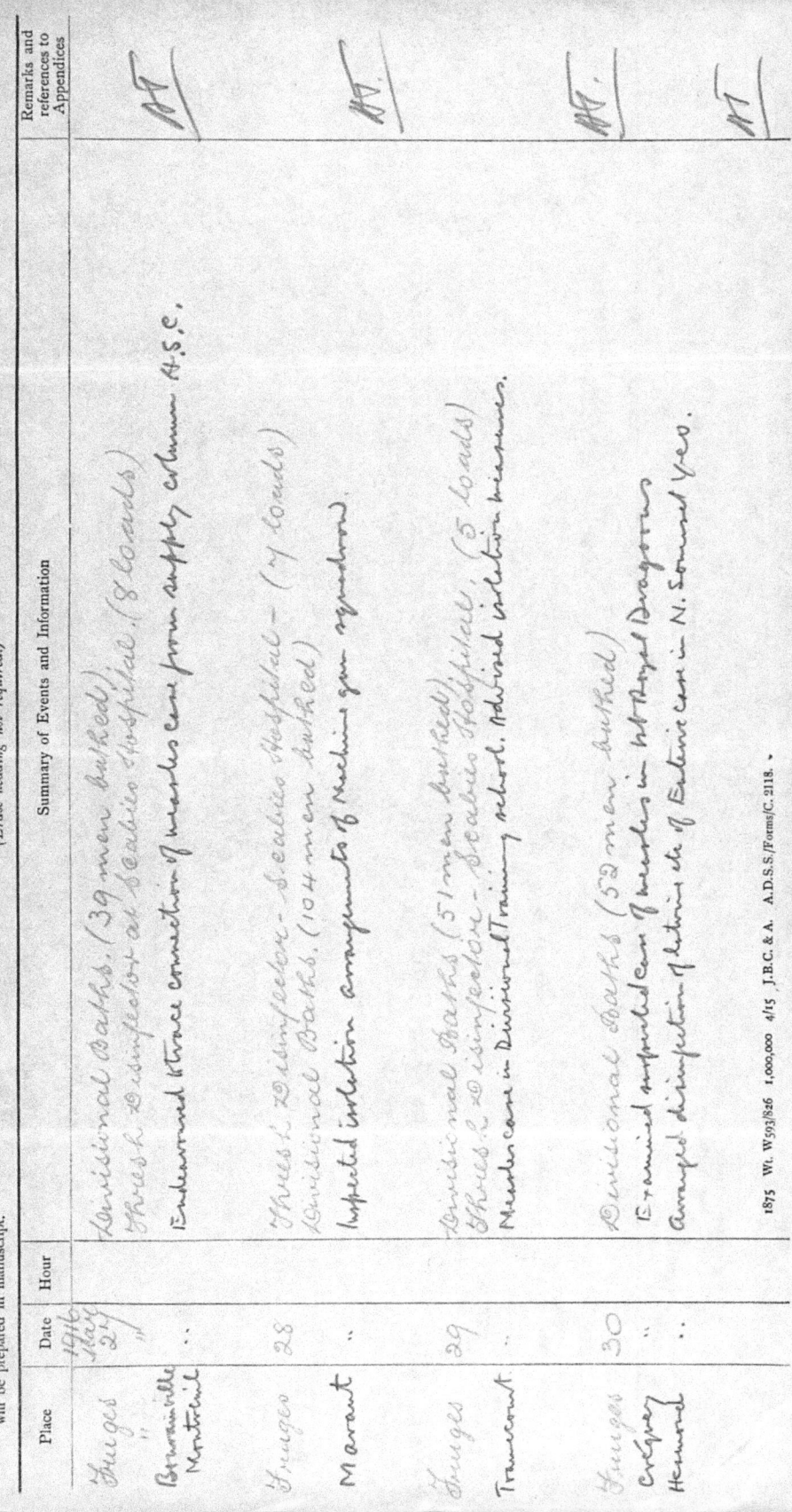

No 12 Section, 2nd London
Sanitary S.O. R.A.M.C.T.F.

Army Form C. 2118

WAR DIARY
or
INTELLIGENCE SUMMARY
(Erase heading not required.)

Instructions regarding War Diaries and Intelligence Summaries are contained in F. S. Regs., Part II. and the Staff Manual respectively. Title Pages will be prepared in manuscript.

Place	Date	Hour	Summary of Events and Information	Remarks and references to Appendices
Hugo Ayr.	1916 Mar 31		Divisional Baths. (31 men bathed) Inspected 6th Brigade H.Q.	
For the Month			1/6 N.C.Os. attached to Regimental Batteries, Brigade H.Q. re-examined the work of superintending the sanitary arrangements of the various units to which they are attached, also disinfecting (during the latter part of the month) the billets to where cases of infectious diseases had occurred.	AT.

[SANITARY SECTION stamp May 1916 THIRD CAVALRY DIV.]

A.C.C. Thompson
Capt.

No. 12. Sanitary Section

Vol 15 - 16 +17
Army Form C. 2118
+ 18

No 12 Section 2nd London
Sanitary Co. R.A.M.C. T.F.

WAR DIARY
or
INTELLIGENCE SUMMARY
(Erase heading not required.)

Instructions regarding War Diaries and Intelligence
Summaries are contained in F. S. Regs., Part II.
and the Staff Manual respectively. Title Pages
will be prepared in manuscript.

THIRD CAVALRY DIV.
SANITARY SECTION

Place	Date 1916	Hour	Summary of Events and Information	Remarks and references to Appendices
Fruges	April	1	Divisional Baths (Establishment and huts cleaned) - Thresh Disinfecting at Seabies Hospital - 6 Beds - (18 particles)	M.T.
Fruges Verchocq Rumilly	"	2	General routine. Inspected M.I.R Guards billets latrines cookhouses etc	M.T.
Fruges	"	3	Divisional Baths (27 men bathed) - Instructing 48th Light Armoured Cars in the building of an Incinerator & digging Latrines etc, - 30 gals petrol tins taken on loan to 2nd Life Guards for use at Latrines buckets. Inspected 2nd L/G Guards billets latrines cookhouses etc.	M.T.
Wicquinghen	"	4	Divisional Baths (45 men bathed)	M.T.
Fruges	"	5	Divisional Baths (8 men bathed) - Thresh Disinfecting at Seabies Hospital 5 to ashes (136 articles)	M.T.

1875. Wt. W593/826 1,000,000 4/15 J.B.C. & A. A.D.S.S./Forms/C. 2118.

WAR DIARY
or
INTELLIGENCE SUMMARY

(Erase heading not required.)

Army Form C. 2118

Instructions regarding War Diaries and Intelligence Summaries are contained in F. S. Regs., Part II. and the Staff Manual respectively. Title Pages will be prepared in manuscript.

[SANITARY SECTION — THIRD CAVALRY DIV. stamp]

Place	Date 1916	Hour	Summary of Events and Information	Remarks and references to Appendices
Bruges	April	6	Divisional Baths (+3 men bathed).	
Air-en-front			Inspected Royal Horse Guards billets etc. at house st.	MT
Bruges	"	7	Divisional Baths. 21 men bathed. Fresh Disinfecting at Seabro Hospital	
Bruges	"	8	Divisional Baths (cleaning rooms, bathers).	MT
Bruges Hooly Bellum	"	9	Disinfection of blankets, kits &c. at Seabro Hospital by means of Thresh Disinfector. Inspected Vicarta Yeomanry billets.	MT

1875 Wt. W593/826 1,000,000 4/15 J.B.C. & A. A.D.S.S./Forms/C. 2118.

WAR DIARY
or
INTELLIGENCE SUMMARY

(Erase heading not required)

Army Form C. 2118

Instructions regarding War Diaries and Intelligence Summaries are contained in F. S. Regs., Part II. and the Staff Manual respectively. Title Pages will be prepared in manuscript.

[Stamp: SANITARY SECTION — THIRD CAVALRY DIV.]

Place	Date 1916	Hour	Summary of Events and Information	Remarks and references to Appendices
Fruges	April 10		Lorry saw off at 10. Entry taking 1400 to Essex Yeo for duty, leaving 2 bottles formalin for disinfecting, to One-en-Gosant with formalin for Rifles, and to Leicester Yeo (Robecq) with 38 hrs for bed as latrine buckets. Divisional Baths, 60 men bathed. Examined suspected case of para-enteric in Supply Column. Examined suspected case of mumps in the 2nd Dragoon Guards.	PT. PT.
Fruges	" 11		Divisional Baths, 74 men bathed. Disinfection by means of Thresh Disinfector at Scabies Hospital blankets, kits, & c. of them 79 R.S. & Scabies Ward & Beds of 6th Cav. Fld. Amb. Total no. of articles 232. Disinfecting bedding of one man at 79 R.S. by means of spray and formalin. Ex-one disinfector taken down & packed ready for transporting to 4th Cav. Field Amb.	NT.
Fruges Huguelines Rollez	" 12		Divisional Baths 6 men bathed. Ex-one disinfector taken to 4th Cav. Field Ambulance & freed up for the use. Examined trace mare of mumps upstairs in Licula, Germany.	NT.
Fruges	" 13		Divisional Baths. (35 men bathed) Disinfection (by means of Thresh Disinfector) of 274 blankets for "B" Squadron North Somerset Yeo, also of 16 articles of clothing, 14 blankets, & kits & one bundle of linen for Scabies Hospital 9 & R.S.	PT.

WAR DIARY
or
INTELLIGENCE SUMMARY

(Erase heading not required.)

Army Form C. 2118

Instructions regarding War Diaries and Intelligence Summaries are contained in F. S. Regs., Part II. and the Staff Manual respectively. Title Pages will be prepared in manuscript.

[STAMP: SANITARY SECTION — THIRD CAVALRY DIV.]

Place	Date 1916	Hour	Summary of Events and Information	Remarks and references to Appendices
Fruges	April 14		Divisional Baths, 24 men bathed.	
Fruges Hinincourt	" 15		Divisional Baths, cleaning up (baths thrown). Disinfecting by means of Spray & formalin 1 large mess room, 1 laughs mess 1 room (small) used as Sleeping quarters, one bath and medical Inspection room of Divisional School.	
Fruges	" "		Disinfection (by means of Thresh Disinfector) of 69 blankets of the 4th Batty; Light Armoured Cars, and 25 miscellaneous articles (12 blankets) for Scabul Hospital.	05
Fruges	" 16		General routine.	
Fruges Embry	" 17		Divisional Baths, 19 men bathed. 1 instigated source of measles case in Essy Germany.	05

WAR DIARY
or
INTELLIGENCE SUMMARY
(Erase heading not required.)

Army Form C.2118

Place	Date	Hour	Summary of Events and Information	Remarks and references to Appendices
Fringes	April 1916 18		10 Divisional Baths, 70 men bathed. Disinfecting (by means of Thresh Disinfector) at Scabies Hospital. 4 loads. Total number of articles, 163. (32 for Scabies Hospital, 95 for 29th Rest Station and 36 for Sanitary Section). Disinfecting (by means of Spray Formolin) at Divisional Rest Station. Investigated source of infection of civilian car resident pus.	AT.
Prichne				
Fringes Prichne	" 19		10 Divisional Baths, 51 men bathed. Disinfecting with Spray Formolin, at a house occupied by H.Q.s A Sqdn 1st Royal Dragoons, and bedroom available by guest suffering from scarlet fever.	111
Fringes	" 20		10 Divisional Baths, 70 men bathed.	
Fringes Prichne Merles	" 21		10 Divisional Baths, 38 men bathed. Disinfection by means of Thresh Disinfector, 131 articles (approx:) for Scabies Hospital and Divisional Rest Station. Investigated source of infection of Enteric case in Royal Horse Guards	AT

WAR DIARY
or
INTELLIGENCE SUMMARY
(Erase heading not required.)

Army Form 'C.' 2118

Instructions regarding War Diaries and Intelligence Summaries are contained in F.S. Regs., Part II. and the Staff Manual respectively. Title Pages will be prepared in manuscript.

SANITARY SECTION
No.........
Date.........
THIRD CAVALRY DIV.

Place	Date 1916	Hour	Summary of Events and Information	Remarks and references to Appendices
Bruges Rinsel	April 22		General routine. Investigated nurses in putting civilian death from Scarlet Fever.	AT
Bruges	" 23		Disinfection (Thresh Disinfector) of 177 articles, comprised of 111 blankets and 4 Ambulances for No 4 Canadian Cavalry Fld Amb. remainder for Sealies Hospital.	AT
Bruges	" 24		Lorry, with an NCO of No 12 San Sec, left for duty at 3rd Dragoon Except to Lomm. Blankets 46 to Berlin for disinfection at G.H.Q. in Sulphur chamber. Thresh Disinfector, disinfection of 82 articles (71 blankets & 11 other articles) for 1st Royal Dragoons. Divisional Baths, 62 men bathed. Steamed inspected car 7 wumps in Supply Column.	AT
Braninville				
Bruges	" 25		Divisional Baths, 82 men bathed. Disinfection of 3 H.Q. articles by means of Thresh Disinfector 144 blankets for Royal Dragoons, 185 articles (including 2 blankets (4) for 10 R.D., R.B. & 9 blankets & light order quilts for Sealies Hospital. Lorry conveying 106 blankets of 3rd D. & 10 Cav. Bde Resvlin to be disinfected in Sulphur chamber returning same after disinfection.	AT

WAR DIARY
or
INTELLIGENCE SUMMARY

Army Form C. 2118

(Erase heading not required.)

[Stamp: SANITARY SECTION — THIRD CAVALRY DIV.]

Instructions regarding War Diaries and Intelligence Summaries are contained in F.S. Regs., Part II. and the Staff Manual respectively. Title Pages will be prepared in manuscript.

Place	Date 1916 April	Hour	Summary of Events and Information	Remarks and references to Appendices
Yvringes		26	Divisional Baths, 10 men bathed. Thresh Disinfector at Seaforts Hospital. Disinfection of 11 blankets, 5 prs & 4 other article for Seaforts Hospital. 6 blankets & 15 other articles for	AT
Coffin			Divisional Rest Station and 8 blankets for "B" Sqdn, 1st Royal Dgns. Contains 225 blankets to besain, brushing in the disinfection and by Sulphide for another Trawning Samel to Regiment, (3rd Dgn Guards).	
Yvringes		27	Divisional Baths, 54 men bathed. Thresh Disinfector at Seaforts Hospital. Disinfecting 106 blankets for 1st R.Dgns, 66 blankets for No 6 Con C.S, and 18se for Seaforts Hospital. Lorry conveying 196 blankets of 3rd Dgds to besain to be disinfected in Sulphur-box Dufor at the door. Also, assisting in the disinfection & returning	AT
Brenninville			and after show/action to the Regiment. Inspected camp ravards in Epping Ground	
Yvringes		28	Divisional Baths, 64 men bathed. Thresh Disinfector at Seaforts Hospital. Disinfection of 226 blankets for North Somerset Yeo., 85 articles for Seaforts Hospital & 16 articles for new Rest Station.	AT
Hesdin			40 blankets conveyed by lorry from office for 3rd Dgn Gds and disinfected by means of the Foden lorry thresh disinfector returned to the Regiment. Lorry returned to its own unit.	
Fressin			Inspected billets etc. of York Shire Dragoons a Cyclist company	AT

No.12 Section 2nd London
Sanitary Co. Ramit. J.

Army Form C. 2118

WAR DIARY
or
INTELLIGENCE SUMMARY
(Erase heading not required.)

Instructions regarding War Diaries and Intelligence Summaries are contained in F. S. Regs., Part II. and the Staff Manual respectively. Title Pages will be prepared in manuscript.

[Stamp: SANITARY SECTION No........ THIRD CAVALRY DIV.]

Place	Date 1916	Hour	Summary of Events and Information	Remarks and references to Appendices
Frugès	April 29		Cleaning up Divisional Baths. Three Disinfectors at Seabies Hospital. Disinfection of 271 blankets for "b" Squadron North Somerset Yeo, 53 articles for Seabies Hospital and 12 articles for Div. Rest Station. Multiple pediculosis meals in Ever Evening.	OK
Enbry	"			
Frugès	"	30	Divisional Baths. 9 men bathed. Three Disinfectors at Seabies Hospital disinfecting 129 articles. Inspected garargrid trianipot lice cases among Canadian and Divisional Schort.	
Transcnt.				
For the month of April			The 16 N.C.O's attached to Regiments, Batteries and Brigade Headquarters continued their work of supervising the sanitary arrangements of the various units to which they are attached. Also disinfecting by means of spray of formalin, after 23 cases of infectious diseases amongst the Division.	

M.L. Thumpon Capt.
O.C. No.12 Section
2nd Lon: San: Co. R. amt. J.T.
attached 3rd Cavalry Division.

No 12 Section, 2nd Cav: San: Co: Rome ? J.?

WAR DIARY
or
INTELLIGENCE SUMMARY
(Erase heading not required.)

Army Form C. 2118

Instructions regarding War Diaries and Intelligence Summaries are contained in F. S. Regs., Part II. and the Staff Manual respectively. Title Pages will be prepared in manuscript.

[Stamp: SANITARY SECTION ✶ THIRD CAVALRY DIV.]

Place	Date 1916	Hour	Summary of Events and Information	Remarks and references to Appendices
Fruges	May 1		Divisional Baths 65 men bathed. Thrush Disinfector at Scabies Hospital. Disinfecting 22 blankets for Gen: M.T. Coy. A.S.C. 64 blankets for Dir: Sehnd. 109 articles for Scabies Hospital and 43 articles for 70a? Rest Station	AT
Fruges	" 2		Divisional Baths 68 men bathed. Thrush Disinfector at Scabies Hospital. Disinfection of 15 blankets & 81 articles of underclothing for 3rd Field Squadron. 2 articles for Divisional Rest Station & 63 articles for Scabies Hospital. Inspected R. Battery R.H.A. billets etc.	AT
Arrival				
Fruges	" 3		Divisional Baths 31 men bathed. Thrush Disinfection at Scabies Hospital. Disinfection of 43 articles for Scabies Hospital & for Divisional Rest Station & 372 blankets & other articles for "C" Battery R.H.A.	
Capelle Mme			Inspected billets of 9 Field Squadron R.E.	
Fruges	" 4		Divisional Baths 33 men bathed. Thrush Disinfection at Scabies Hospital. disinfecting 40 articles for Scabies Hospital and 169 articles for "G" Battery R.H.A.	AT

WAR DIARY
or
INTELLIGENCE SUMMARY
(Erase heading not required.)

Army Form C. 2118

Instructions regarding War Diaries and Intelligence Summaries are contained in F. S. Regs., Part II. and the Staff Manual respectively. Title Pages will be prepared in manuscript.

[Stamp: SANITARY SECTION – THIRD CAVALRY DIV.]

Place	Date 1916	Hour	Summary of Events and Information	Remarks and references to Appendices
Fruges	May 5		Divisional Baths, 27 men bathed.	
Fruges	" 6		Divisional Baths. Cleaning up. Thresh Disinfector at Scabies Hospital, disinfecting 61 articles for Scabies Hospital, and 243 articles for Ammunition Park.	67
"	" 7		General routine.	
"	" 8		Divisional baths, 51 men bathed. Thresh-Disinfector at Scabies Hospital, disinfecting 353 articles for Ammunition Column (R.H.A.). 30 articles for Scabies Hospital + 2 ovencles for R.H.S. G/S Wagon belonging to Amn Col. conveying articles disinfected by means of Thresh Spray. Lorry conveying to Heidin 244 articles for disinfection.	68
Fruges	" 9		Divisional baths, 59 men bathed. Thresh Disinfector at Scabies Hospital disinfecting 22 gaskets for Amn Col, 14 articles for N/B LA.D, 634 for Scabies Hospital.	69
Humbert	" "		Disinfecting by means of Spray Formalin, 2 rooms at billet of N/B L.A.D. Lorry journey to Heidin conveying 243 blankets of 10th Hussars for disinfection.	
Fullen	" "		Disinfecting Wells of Yorkshire Dragoons (Spray N formalin)	

WAR DIARY or INTELLIGENCE SUMMARY

(Erase heading not required.)

Army Form C. 2118

Place	Date	Hour	Summary of Events and Information	Remarks and references to Appendices
Fruges	1916 May 10		Divisional Baths 21 men bathed. Thresh Disinfector at Scabies Hospital, disinfecting 407 articles for 1st Life Guards, 21 articles for Scabies Hospital.	
Humbert	"		Lorry journey 240 blankets of 10 R.H. for disinfection at Hesdin.	
Fruges	"	11	Divisional Baths, 41 men bathed. Thresh Disinfector at Scabies Hospital, disinfecting 295 articles for 1st Life Guards 55 articles for Scabies Hospital & 40 for 10 R.H.	M.T
Humbert Hulmarque	" "		Lorry journey to Hesdin conveying 46 blankets for disinfection. Billet of Leics Yeo. sprayed out with Izool/100 cas. of Infectious Disease.	
Fruges	"	12	Divisional Baths 20 men bathed. Thresh Disinfector at Scabies Hospital, disinfecting 135 articles for Scabies Hospital, 32 arts for 10 R.H.	M.T
Fruges	"	13	Divisional Baths. Cole aunsupl. General routine.	
Fruges	"	14	All N.C.O. & men required section from Regiments. Thresh disinfector at Scabies Hospital, disinfecting 209 articles for Scabies Hospital	M.T

WAR DIARY or INTELLIGENCE SUMMARY

(Erase heading not required.)

Army Form C. 2118

Instructions regarding War Diaries and Intelligence Summaries are contained in F. S. Regs., Part II. and the Staff Manual respectively. Title Pages will be prepared in manuscript.

SANITARY SECTION — THIRD CAVALRY DIV.

Place	Date	Hour	Summary of Events and Information	Remarks and references to Appendices
Fruges Maison Fontheu	1916 May 15		Left Fruges barn for Maison Fontheu. Returned 7.30 pm. Cleaning & spraying out Mairie, one closet pernail & an outbuilding. Cleaning out old straw, turning same, cleaning out & spraying rooms over School, one room on ground floor. Staircase & cellar. Cleaning out old straw, turning same, also spraying large Barn recently occupied by Indian troops. — Rigging latrines at rear, having been made of tarry 500 bricks, and constructing an incinerator in a central place for general use. Also digging pit for burnt rubbish. of A.S.C. & Supplies. Small stores occupied by men. Sprayed out. Latrines behind Signal office. One room to be occupied by a S.O. sprayed out. Latrines for O.S. Officers mess. Stable sprayed out. Commandant's horses sprayed out.	NT
Fruges	"	16	Divisional Baths 24 men bathed.	
Gommecourt	"	"	Chateau:— on top floor, shaking carpets, cleaning out fireplaces, cleaning up Burning rubbish, washing under buckets. Dusting out & dusting W. bedroom & closets (including one WC) landing & staircase. On 2nd floor same procedure on 6 rooms, 5 closets (including one WC) landing & staircase. Ground floor, same procedure in 4 rooms & hall & passage.	NT

WAR DIARY
or
INTELLIGENCE SUMMARY

(Erase heading not required.)

Army Form C. 2118

Instructions regarding War Diaries and Intelligence Summaries are contained in F. S. Regs., Part II. and the Staff Manual respectively. Title Pages will be prepared in manuscript.

[Stamp: SANITARY SECTION — THIRD CAVALRY DIV.]

Place	Date 1916.	Hour	Summary of Events and Information	Remarks and references to Appendices
Fruges	May 14		Divisional Baths, 22 men bathed. Thresh Disinfector, disinfecting 87 articles for Scabies Hospital & 35 for D.R.S.	AT
Schquen	"		Disinfecting by means of Spray Formalin, after German measles, part of a Billet.	NT
Fruges	"	18	Divisional Baths, 35 men bathed.	NT
Fruges	"	19	Divisional Baths, 19 men bathed. Thresh Disinfector, disinfecting 124 articles for Scabies Hospital and 18 for D.R.S.	
Argenvillers	"		Disinfecting after German measles, by means of Spray & Formalin part of a barn, burned straw, disinfected bed & surroundings. 15 sey Germans	BT
Fruges	"	20	General routine.	
Conchy	"		Disinfecting after German measles (R.H.Ads.) Sprayed with Formalin part of a barn.	NT

WAR DIARY
or
INTELLIGENCE SUMMARY

Place	Date	Hour	Summary of Events and Information	Remarks and references to Appendices
Bruges	1916 May 21		General routine.	
"	"	22	Divisional Baths, 38 men bathed.	M
Canton St Martin	"		Disinfecting by means of Spray formalin part of a barn, after evacuation of sick & wounded.	
Flambeau	"		Cleaning out & disinfecting 2 rooms for Signallers, at Chateau, & digging latrines.	
Bruges	"		Thresh Disinfector disinfecting 74 articles for Scabies Hospital, 25 for LRS & Sani. Sec.	M
Bruges	"	23	Divisional Baths, 21 men bathed.	
Humbeaur	"		Party cleaning room, landing, staircase & c at Chateau - also grounds & courtyard. Lorry & lorry to Huguelien & spray with 30 hrs for 2nd Life Guards. Sewing up covered latrine for mail at Chateau.	M
Bruges	"	24	Divisional Baths, 3 men bathed.	M

WAR DIARY or INTELLIGENCE SUMMARY

Army Form C. 2118

(Erase heading not required.)

Instructions regarding War Diaries and Intelligence Summaries are contained in F.S. Regs., Part II. and the Staff Manual respectively. Title Pages will be prepared in manuscript.

[Stamp: SANITARY SECTION — THIRD CAVALRY DIV.]

Place	Date 1916	Hour	Summary of Events and Information	Remarks and references to Appendices
Hingee	May 25		Divisional baths, 7 men bathed. Fricot Disinfectah Scabies Hospital. Disinfecting 153 articles for Scabies Hospital & 44 for D.P.Shr.	AF
Crecey Remilly Impies Hingee	"		Disinfecting by means of Serry formalin, a mess room & small bedroom at the Elso-Dieck de Gaufe. Disinfected 16 WR & F. goods. 5 ruined civilian cases of diphtheria & one case of diphtheria carrier. Disposed all used supplies & private property in piste.	
	"	26	Divisional Baths. 8 men bathed. Disposed water carts of 8th C.F.A.	
Rainbert Duntraine Aquancourt Hingee			" " " Esser Yeomanry N.S. Yeomanry	
	"	27	General routine.	
Murgaline Ruilen Appro bount	"		Disposed water carts of 7th C.F.A. and 3rd Brigade H.Q. Disposed cans of horses in Royal Horse Guards & one installment.	
Hingee	"	28	Fricot Disinfector at Scabies Hospital – Disinfecting 99 articles for Scabies Hospital. 48 articles for D.P.S. & 35 for Battalions.	AF
Bondues			Disposed interior of private Yeomanry	
Hingee	"	29	Divisional Baths. 20 men bathed. Lorry journey to Heymond (N.S.yeo) leaving 50 ans to Fourgueliens. Following truck dose disinfectors to Bouvikes leaving 25 Ans with Leicester Yeomanry.	AF
Ontia			Found nettable water supply for the D.R.S.	

No 12 Section 2nd Lor Sanitary Co
Rame.I.f.

Army Form C. 2118

Instructions regarding War Diaries and Intelligence Summaries are contained in F. S. Regs, Part II. and the Staff Manual respectively. Title Pages will be prepared in manuscript.

WAR DIARY
or
INTELLIGENCE SUMMARY
(Erase heading not required.)

[Stamp: SANITARY SECTION — THIRD CAVALRY DIV.]

Place	Date	Hour	Summary of Events and Information	Remarks and references to Appendices
Forges Pierval	1916 May 30		Divisional baths. 28 men bathed. Instructed orderlies men and M.O. on 98 th Brigade in use of water testing apparatus.	AF
Forges	" 31		Divisional baths. 11 men bathed. Inspected N.S. Verrines billets latrines etc.	
Hermonville Liverrines	For the month of May 1916.		The 16 N.C.Os attached to Regiments, Batteries & Brigade Headquarters continued their work of supervising the sanitary arrangements of the various units to which they are attached.	

M.W. Thompson
Capt R.A.M.C.
O.C. No 12 Sanitary Section
2nd London San: Coy:Rame S.T.
attached 3rd Cavalry Division

L.G.J.

12th Sanitary Section

COMMITTEE FOR THE
MEDICAL HISTORY OF THE WAR
Date 13 SEP. 1915

No 12 Section 2nd Lori, Samp. Bo. Ra. m.c. J.F. WAR DIARY or INTELLIGENCE SUMMARY

Army Form C. 2118

(Erase heading not required.)

SANITARY SECTION
No.............
Date...........
THIRD CAVALRY DIV.

Place	Date	Hour	Summary of Events and Information	Remarks and references to Appendices
Fruges	June 1916	1	Divisional Baths. 11 men bathed. Lorry journey fetching 100 petrol tins from Supply Column. Imported into camp C Betting.	AT
Wavrans				
Fruges	"	2	Divisional Baths 15 men bathed. Lorry Journey to 9 1st Life Guards with tins for latrines. Imported into camp 9 Betting M.H.A.	AT
Fruges Bruthen	"	3	Divisional Baths, cleaning up. Disinfection (by steam) of 150 articles for Scabies Hospital. Imported into Yemmy camps.	AT
Fruges	"	4	General routine	
"	"	5	General routine. Divisional Baths 3 men bathed.	
"	"	6	General routine	
"	"	7	Lorry journey to CONTES with load of bricks for 19 Div. Rest Stn.	AT
"	"	8	Lorry journey to Contes with bricks & 3 zinc baths from 19 Div Baths	AT

WAR DIARY
or
INTELLIGENCE SUMMARY
(Erase heading not required.)

Army Form C. 2118

Instructions regarding War Diaries and Intelligence Summaries are contained in F.S. Regs., Part II. and the Staff Manual respectively. Title Pages will be prepared in manuscript.

Place	Date	Hour	Summary of Events and Information	Remarks and references to Appendices
Bruges Coupelle Neuve	1916 June	9	Lorry journey to Conkes with Bathhouse equipment for use by 19th R.H.Sm. Inspected 2nd Field Squadron R.E.	M
Fosser Coupelle Vieille	"	10	Lorry journey to Conkes. Inspected Ammunition Column	M
Fosser Aubry	"	11	Lorry journey to 10 R.B.sm, Conkes. Inspected K battery.	
Fosser Sempy	"	12	Thresh Disinfector left Leaders Hospital for 10 R.Sm. at Conkes. Lorry journey to Conkes with boell for Disinfector. Inspected 17th Hussars	M
Fosser	"	13	General routine.	
Embry	"	14	General routine. Inspected 15 Essex Yeomanry.	M
"	"	15	Lorry journey to X R.Hussars at Sempy with 30 petrol tins for use as latrines. To Bouquehault, Luesser yeo to convey blankets to for disinfection at Middlin on following day. Inspected Royal Horse Guards.	
Fauvin				

WAR DIARY
or
INTELLIGENCE SUMMARY

(Erase heading not required.)

Army Form C. 2118

Place	Date	Hour	Summary of Events and Information	Remarks and references to Appendices
Bruges Louvain (Beverloo)	1916 June 16		Lorry journey from Bruges to Hasselin with 501 blankets of Leicester Yeo. for disinfection at Cavalry Barracks. Inspected 2nd Bryom guards.	105
Fiper	"	17	General routine.	107
"	"	18	General routine. Inspected camp 7 ind L.G. guards	
Niz-en-Croy	"	19	General routine.	
Fiper	"	20	General routine.	
"	"	21	Lorry journey to Cortes, B.R.S reporting 6.30 for duty following day.	107
"	"	22	Lorry journey from Cortes to Bruges with both equipment and on to St Omer with Surplus medical Stores & Equipment for handing over to D.R.L.S.	105

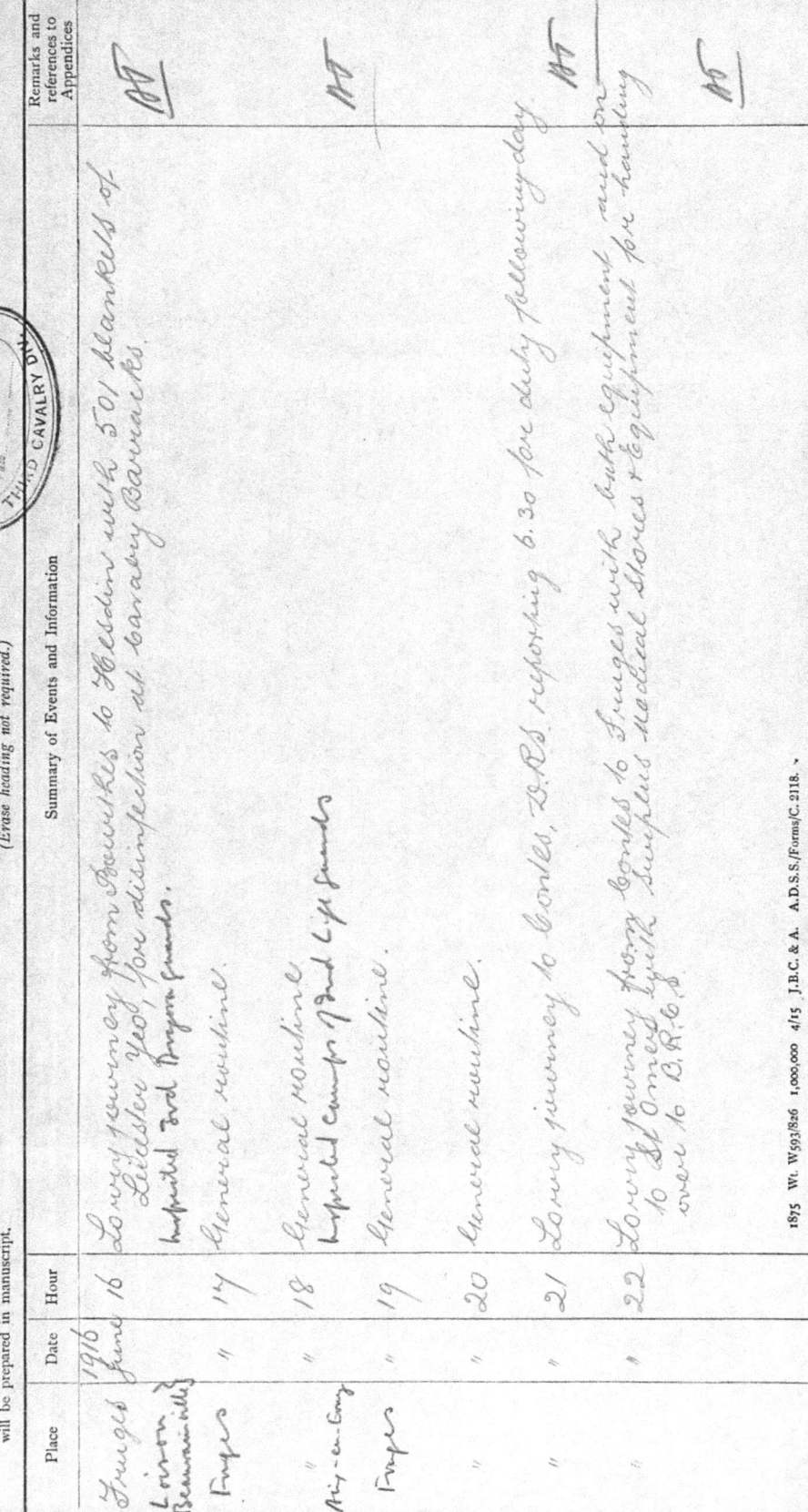

WAR DIARY
or
INTELLIGENCE SUMMARY

(Erase heading not required.)

Army Form C. 2118

Place	Date 1916	Hour	Summary of Events and Information	Remarks and references to Appendices
Fauges	June 23		Converting 222 Shelford huts into Latrine Buckets.	M
"	24		Completing the preparation of the huts commenced yesterday. Inspection of town prior to evacuation on following day. All billets, stables and other places occupied by troops handed in clean condition.	
"	25		To DOMART-en-PONTHIEU	
DOMART-en-PONTHIEU	26		To CORBIE (LA NEUVILLE)	
LA NEUVILLE	27		Inspection of lodgings & cooperators with Town-major & a Sgt. of Sanitary Section (about to visit the town) previously of & of Sanitary arrangements. Foden Steam Lorry (Thresh-Disinfector) joined Section today.	M
"	28		Burning refuse at dump.	M

No. 12 Section 2nd London San. 60 R. amc. T.F.

WAR DIARY
or
INTELLIGENCE SUMMARY.

Army Form C. 2118.

Place	Date	Hour	Summary of Events and Information	Remarks and references to Appendices
	1916			
LA NEUVILLE	June 29		Burying refuse at "Dump".	A
"	" 30		Burning refuse at "Dump"	
	For the Month of June 1916.		The 16 N.C.Os continued their work of supervising the Sanitary arrangements of the Units to which they are attached, moving with the Regiments, etc., when the Division moved from the old billeting area instead of rejoining their own unit.	B

M.C.Thompson
Capt.
O.C. 2nd Sanitary Section

No. 12 Section 2nd Line Line: &c: Ramc. A.F. **WAR DIARY**
or
INTELLIGENCE SUMMARY.

Army Form C. 2118.

(Erase heading not required.)

Place	Date	Hour	Summary of Events and Information	Remarks and references to Appendices
LA NEUVILLE	1916 July	1	Standing by.	
Le Neuville	"	2	Standing by.	A5
Bonnay Le Neuville	"	3	Sealed where Brigades use to the when drinking water was to drawn. Inspection of latrines & reporting on their condition. Emptying officers latrines & burying same. Burning refuse.	A6
Bonnay Le Neuville	"	4	Arranged better manure disposal of Brigades. To Hallencourt.	A6
HALLENCOURT	"	5	Building Incinerator for Divisional Headquarters.	
AIRAINES	"	6	Completed incinerator commenced yesterday & burned refuse. Footer Lorry (Motor Disinfector) disinfecting blankets &c for 6th Cav Bde.	A7

Army Form C. 2118.

No 12 Section, 2nd Lon. San. Co. Rams. T.F.

WAR DIARY
or
INTELLIGENCE SUMMARY.
(Erase heading not required.)

Instructions regarding War Diaries and Intelligence Summaries are contained in F. S. Regs., Part II. and the Staff Manual respectively. Title pages will be prepared in manuscript.

[Stamp: SANITARY SECTION — THIRD CAVALRY DIV.]

Place	Date	Hour	Summary of Events and Information	Remarks and references to Appendices
Hallencourt	1916 July 7		Standing by.	
"	" 8		to Daours.	
Daours	" 9		Repaired incinerators, burned refuse, constructing urinal, digging and making box seat latrines (No 4), for the use of Divisional H. Qrs. and one Brigade of 33rd Inf. Division.	K
Daours	" 10		Burning refuse. Completed latrines (including one for Officers). Repaired some civilian ratios from Major.	
"	" 11		Making further mine bore seats for latrines dug by men of 33rd Division. Assisting as numerators in disposal of refuse. Preparing for channel &c for urinal. Burnt & made.	
"	" 12		Disposal of refuse. Constructing urinal. Digging own latrines	K

No 12 Section 2nd Lon: San: Co. R.A.M.C. T.F. **WAR DIARY** or **INTELLIGENCE SUMMARY.**

Army Form C. 2118.

Instructions regarding War Diaries and Intelligence Summaries are contained in F. S. Regs., Part II. and the Staff Manual respectively. Title pages will be prepared in manuscript.

(Erase heading not required.)

[SANITARY SECTION — THIRD CAVALRY DIV. stamp]

Place	Date	Hour	Summary of Events and Information	Remarks and references to Appendices
	1916			
Lacouture	July 13		Burning & disposal of refuse. Disinfecting latrines & urinals. Digging latrines.	A1
"	" 14		General routine. (Inspection of grounds occupied by Leics Yeo. (for 4yrs)	
"	" 15		Standing to.	
"	" 16		"	A1
Estree Blanche	"		Supplied car to C.S.19. in twenty four. All precautions taken.	
Douvrin	" 17		Standing to. — Thrush Disinfector disinfecting blankets & clothing of 90th Bgde 30th Division.	A5
Pont Niepplen	"		Investigated outbreak of diarrhoea in supply column.	
Douvrin	" 18		Disinfection of 231 blankets of No 8 C.F.A. Inspected Amm. Park camp.	A1

No.12 Section 2nd Lon: San: coy R.A.M.C. A.F.

WAR DIARY
INTELLIGENCE SUMMARY.

Army Form C. 2118.

Place	Date	Hour	Summary of Events and Information	Remarks and references to Appendices
	1916			
Dacours	July 19		Burning refuse and salvaging articles of clothing & equipment left by the 90th Bde 30th Division. Inspection of grounds and buildings after being vacated by this Brigade	AT
Contive			Inspected camp of htrs of grounds of hier Yeo.	
Dacours	" 20		Rebuilding incinerators, reconstructing greasetrap & filling in old ones. Inspection of grounds & buildings occupied by 90th B Bde 30th Div and reporting on the sanitary condition thereof. Thresh Disinfector disinfecting blankets & clothing of 1st Royal Dragoons.	AT
Rainney			Took water from intelligancing of diptheria in Essex Yeo.	AT
Dacours	" 21		Digging latrines & making two box seats for same.	
L'Neuville			Disinfecting blankets of 1st Royal Dgds.	AT

No. 12 Section 2nd London Co. R.a.m.c. A.F.   Army Form C. 2118.

WAR DIARY
or
INTELLIGENCE SUMMARY.

Instructions regarding War Diaries and Intelligence Summaries are contained in F. S. Regs., Part II. and the Staff Manual respectively. Title pages will be prepared in manuscript.

(Erase heading not required.)

Place	Date	Hour	Summary of Events and Information	Remarks and references to Appendices
	1916			
Daours	July 22		Lorry journey to Corbie with case of N.C.O. powder for disinfection amongst the 8th Bgde.	
Corbie			Thrush Disinfector, disinfecting blankets, clothing &c. for 1st Life Gds. Inspected 9th Brigade camp, & Rotting Machine gun, 3rd & 4th Hussars, 2nd Life Guards	M
Daours	23		Lorry journey to Corbie No. 4 Can. Bgde. with sick & c. to Corbie Disinfector. Inspection of grounds occupied by 10th H. Quarter Master Stores field day for 9th Huss.	M
Corbie			Thrush Disinfector, disinfecting at 1st Life Gds.	
Daours	24		Lorry journey to Corbie (No. 4 Can. Bgde.) with conl. 40. Thrush Disinfector, disinfecting outfits for 2nd Life Gds.	
Bronnay			Inspected the whole of the camps of the 8th Bde. Brigade ex-cept the Royal Horse guards.	M

No 12 Section, 2nd London Co: R.A.M.C. T.F.

WAR DIARY
or
INTELLIGENCE SUMMARY.

Army Form C. 2118.

Instructions regarding War Diaries and Intelligence
Summaries are contained in F. S. Regs., Part II.
and the Staff Manual respectively. Title pages
will be prepared in manuscript.

Place	Date	Hour	Summary of Events and Information	Remarks and references to Appendices
	1916			
Dranoutre	July 25		Thresh Disinfector disinfecting blankets & clothing for 2nd Life Gds at Locre	AF
			General routine	
Berney			Inspected Camp of Royal Horse Guards	
Locre	26		Spraying manure heaps alongside main road in field used by 2nd Signal Squadron. Freeing race track over French for Officers Mess, 2nd Signal Sqdrn.	AF
"	"		Disposal of refuse for 12th Bde	
Locre	"		Thresh Disinfector disinfecting blankets, clothing for Divisional yeo:	
La Nieuville			Inspected camp & Billets of 3rd D. Guards & N.S. Yeomanry	
Dranoutre	27		Disposal of refuse for 12th Bde	AF
Berlie			Thresh Disinfector disinfecting for Essex Yeomanry	
La Nieuville			Inspected Royal Horse Guards & 6th machine gun squadron camps	

No.12 Section, 2nd London Co. R.a.m.c. S.F. **WAR DIARY** or **INTELLIGENCE SUMMARY**

Army Form C. 2118.

Place	Date	Hour	Summary of Events and Information	Remarks and references to Appendices
	1916			
Dnours	July 28		General routine	
Corbie	" "		"Thresh"-Disinfector, disinfecting blankets & clothing of "K" Battery R.H.A.	
Fo Neuville				
Corbie			Inspected C. Battery R.H.A.	A
			Inspected 2nd L.F. Guards.	
Dnours	" 29		General routine. Inspected 3rd Field Squadron R.E.	
Corbie	" "		"Thresh" Disinfector, disinfecting blankets & clothing of "J" R.H. Squadron	B
Heneu			tops	
Dnours	" 30		General routine.	
Corbie	" "		Disinfecting blankets & clothing of 3rd C.F.A., N.R.H.S. & 7th C.F.A.	C
Dnours	" 31		General routine.	

For the month of July 1916 the 16 N.C.Os continued the work of supervising the Sanitary arrangements of the Units to which they are attached.

M.L. Thompson
Capt. R.A.M.C.
O.C. No 12 Sanitary Section
3rd Cavalry Division

DIARY of

No 12 Sanitary Section

Month of August 1916

Vol 19

No. 12 Section 2nd London Sanitary Co
Name ? ?

WAR DIARY
or
INTELLIGENCE SUMMARY.
(Erase heading not required.)

Army Form C. 2118.

Instructions regarding War Diaries and Intelligence Summaries are contained in F. S. Regs., Part II. and the Staff Manual respectively. Title pages will be prepared in manuscript.

SANITARY SECTION
No. ....
Date Aug/16
THIRD CAVALRY DIV.

Place	Date 1916	Hour	Summary of Events and Information	Remarks and references to Appendices
Daours	Aug	1	Inspection of Sailing grounds occupied by Divisional Head Quarters. Prior to arrival Inspection of all camping area of the division after it had moved. Left Daours for St Gresnoy	
St Gresnoy	"	2	Left St Gresnoy for Yvrenchense	M
Yvrenchense	"	3	Disinfecting 552 articles for 3rd Dragoon Guards. Lorry journey to St Riquier (Rouchead) two load for Longuenoy	
Yvrenchense	"	4	Move to Longuecourt	
Longuecourt	"	5	Move from Longuecourt to Frunges	
Frunges	"	6	Making Notice boards: "Drinking water", "Washing water", "Additional water" & "unfit for troops". Lorry journey Friday for 3rd Signal Squadron R.E.	M
Frunges	"	7	Lorry journey to Uffier with 5 baths. Stove and 1 ton of coal to 1st London Seam Disinfecting + 63 articles for No. 6 G.F.A. (including Drake & Cohen's Blankets & Clothing) to 1st Sig. Sqns. "C" Sting Hosp. M.S.R.G.A. Bed Lyft. Seld Lorry journey (in the afternoon) to No. 6 G.F.A. Leaving 4-8 hno with each Reg: 2H with Bolly, 4H with Harands. Continuing Notice Board (as commenced yesterday)	AT
Uffier				
Frunges				

WAR DIARY or INTELLIGENCE SUMMARY

Army Form C. 2118.

No. 12 Section, 2nd Low Cum. 60. R.A.M.C. J.F.

Instructions regarding War Diaries and Intelligence Summaries are contained in F. S. Regs., Part II. and the Staff Manual respectively. Title pages will be prepared in manuscript.

(Erase heading not required.)

SANITARY SECTION — THIRD CAVALRY DIV.

Place	Date	Hour	Summary of Events and Information	Remarks and references to Appendices
Fruges	1916 Aug 8		Continued the making & painting of the Notice boards commenced 6th inst. Supervising & assisting in the digging of latrines of topon held occupied by horse lines of 4.4e, of B1by a.J.G, Greys and Carabiniers Drive	A1
Coffin			Disinfecting 1110 articles for 3rd Dragoon Guards.	
Fruges	" 9		Completed Notice boards (as mentioned above) Completed latrines commenced yesterday (as above) Construction Wire pit and grease trap drainage pit for field machine shop.	A1
Coffin			Disinfecting 344 articles for 10 Pro Imc D.Gs, No 6 C.F.A, & 2nd Lt. Sys'm	
Fruges	" 10		Disinfecting 1313 articles for North Somerset Yeo and Library. General routine.	A1
Fruges	" 11		Pumping water from rear of empty house about to be occupied by 3rd Signal squadron, also spraying same, and two rooms apart above. Lorry journey 10 Libion with Cart from Fallen Lorry.	A1
Libion				

T2134. Wt. W708—776. 500000. 4/15. Sir J. C. & S.

No 12 Section 2nd Lon: San: Co: R.A.M.C. T.F. WAR DIARY or INTELLIGENCE SUMMARY.

Army Form C. 2118.

(Erase heading not required.)

Instructions regarding War Diaries and Intelligence Summaries are contained in F. S. Regs., Part II. and the Staff Manual respectively. Title pages will be prepared in manuscript.

[Stamp: SANITARY SECTION No. — Aug 16 — THIRD CAVALRY DIV.]

Place	Date	Hour	Summary of Events and Information	Remarks and references to Appendices
Fruges Lieres	1916 Aug 11		General routine. Disinfecting 888 articles of clothing, blankets &c for North Som Yeo, 13th Hussars. Veterinary Section and Essex Yeo.	A.T.
Fruges	" 12		General routine. Spraying out yard & outhouse adjoining the empty house to be used as a Guardhouse & Mess Room by the 3rd Signal Sqdrn. Constructing incinerator for Divisional H.Qrs at Framecourt.	A.T.
Royon	"		Disinfecting 392 articles of clothing & for 6th Can: Regt: H. Yrs & H.Qrs N.S. Yeo.	A.T.
Fruges & Framecourt	" 13		Lorry journey to Framecourt with party & incinerator for fixing at Div: H.Q. Erecting same & instructing sanitary orderly in method & sanitary arrangements	
Fruges	"		Constructing another incinerator for field occupied by 81 Coy A.S.C. & erecting same.	
Lignereuil Gournay	"		Disinfecting 1598 articles for 6th Machine Gun Sqdrn.	A.T.

Army Form C. 2118.

No 12 Section 2nd London Sanitary Section WAR DIARY or INTELLIGENCE SUMMARY.

Instructions regarding War Diaries and Intelligence Summaries are contained in F. S. Regs., Part II. and the Staff Manual respectively. Title pages will be prepared in manuscript.

(Erase heading not required.)

SANITARY SECTION No. Army 16 THIRD CAVALRY DIV.

Place	Date	Hour	Summary of Events and Information	Remarks and references to Appendices
	1916			
Fruges	Aug 14		Lorry journey to 3rd Canton Supply Column Workshops for re-tyreing. The tyres considered not sufficiently worn & returned same day.	
Nordausques			Disinfecting 583 articles of Clothing &c for "C" Batty R.H.A. & H.Qrs. 6th Cav Bgde.	M.
Fruges			Foden lorry returned to HQrs. for coal & proceeded to 8th Cav Bgde. following day.	
Fruges	"	15	Foden lorry (Disinfector) proceeded to commence disinfection at 8th Cav Bgde.	
Tenour	"		Disinfecting 216 articles of Clothing &c for Royal Horse Guards.	M.
Fruges	"	16	General routine.	
Tenour & Erin			Disinfecting 265 articles for Royal Horse Guards & 8th Cav Bgde HQrs.	M.
Fruges Erin	"	17	General routine. Inspection of 1st Royal Dragoons.	M.

T.J.134. Wt. W708—776. 500000. 4/15. Sir J. C. & S.

No. 2 Section 2nd London No. Corps C.J. **WAR DIARY** or **INTELLIGENCE SUMMARY**

Army Form C. 2118.

(Erase heading not required.)

Instructions regarding War Diaries and Intelligence Summaries are contained in F.S. Regs., Part II. and the Staff Manual respectively. Title pages will be prepared in manuscript.

SANITARY SECTION
No. ....
Date Aug 16
THIRD CAVALRY DIV.

Place	Date	Hour	Summary of Events and Information	Remarks and references to Appendices
	1916			
Fouges	Aug 18		Lorry journey to Montreuil with Coal for Foden Steam lorry.	
Blangy			Disinfecting 1000 articles of Clothing for "A" Sqn Essex Yeo	AT
Auchy-les-Hesdin			Inspection of 10th Hussars.	
Fruges		19	General routine	
Blangy			Disinfecting 426 articles for Essex Yeo "B" Sqdn.	
Transcount			Inspection of Divisional fuel gratis	
Fruges		20	Lorry journey to Crini & Blingel to H.Qrs 8th Cav Bgde. 4 Foden lorry	
Blingel			Disinfecting 308 articles for 8th C.F.A. & Mobile Vet. Section	AT
Fruges		21	Inspection of field horse lines of 4th Yrs Details (horse lines) Police & 81 Coy A.S.C.	
Ruchy Erudy Rogers			Disinfecting 916 articles for 10th Royal Hussars. Inspected (a grande H.Q. Inspected N.S. Yeomanry	AT
Fruges		22	General routine	
Auchy			Disinfecting 2100 articles for 10th R. Hussars	AT
Beuthes			Inspected Leicester Yeomanry	AT

No. 2 Section, 2nd Lon. San. Coy. R.A.M.C.

WAR DIARY
or
INTELLIGENCE SUMMARY.
(Erase heading not required.)

Army Form C. 2118.

Instructions regarding War Diaries and Intelligence
Summaries are contained in F. S. Regs., Part II.
and the Staff Manual respectively. Title pages
will be prepared in manuscript.

Place	Date	Hour	Summary of Events and Information	Remarks and references to Appendices
Fruges	1916 Aug 23		Lorry journey to HQrs 8th Cav Bgde R HQrs ¾ Disinfecting Foundry Lorry journey to Dromfore (in afternoon) with coal.	
Auchy Bondus	"		Disinfecting 577 articles of Clothing &c for 8th Machine Gun Sqdn. Abandoned potatoes in kitchen with contents of a can of S.F. in biscuit. Yeomanry Norgn. Junction Caulkfred	AT
Fruges Grigny	" 24		Jordan Lorry returned to 19in HQrs after completing disinfection of 8th Cav Bgde, finishing with "G" Suchy 8th Bgde 309 articles.	AT
Fruges Auchy Fruges	" 25 " 26		General routine. Inspected the N.S. Yeomanry General routine. Lorry journey to Cochinsent (stopped en route) with a party of men from 6 Bd 4th 6 Jul.	AT
Fruges	" 27		General routine.	AT

Army Form C. 2118

No. 12 Sanitary Section, 2nd London (C.O.) Regt., WAR DIARY or INTELLIGENCE SUMMARY.

(Erase heading not required.)

Instructions regarding War Diaries and Intelligence Summaries are contained in F. S. Regs., Part II. and the Staff Manual respectively. Title pages will be prepared in manuscript.

Place	Date	Hour	Summary of Events and Information	Remarks and references to Appendices
	1916			
Fruges	Aug 28		Repairing latrines at field occupied by 81 Coy A.S.C.	
Eaville	"	"	Disinfecting 1143 missiles for Divisional Ammunition Column.	
Fruges	"	29	General routine.	
Torcy	"	"	Disinfecting 346 vehicles for 3rd Field Squadron R.E.	
Crémecourt	"	"	Spraying with formalin Signal Office & Harness store adjoining.	
Fruges	Aug 30		Disinfection of 413 for the 16 Vrs A.S.C., 3rd Squad. Sqn R.E. Amn. Park & 9th Light Amn. Park.	
			Journeyed to Hesdin taking a motor cycle having a broken axle in to Divisional workshops for repairs.	
Fruges	"	31	General routine.	
			For the Month of August 1916. The 15 N.C.Os continued their routine work of supervising & inspecting the sanitary arrangements of the units to which they are attached.	

M. Thornton
V.C. Capt RAMC
No. 12 Sanitary Section
3rd Cavalry Division

140/189

3rd Cav Div

12th Sanitary Section

Sept. 1916.

COMMITTEE FOR THE
MEDICAL HISTORY OF THE WAR
Date -2 DEC. 1916

No 20

Diary of
No 12 Sanitary Section
September 1916

No 12 Section 2nd London Sanitary Coy R.A.M.C.

WAR DIARY
or
INTELLIGENCE SUMMARY.

Army Form C. 2118.

Instructions regarding War Diaries and Intelligence Summaries are contained in F. S. Regs., Part II. and the Staff Manual respectively. Title pages will be prepared in manuscript.

(Erase heading not required.)

Place	Date	Hour	Summary of Events and Information	Remarks and references to Appendices
	1916			
Fruges	Sept 1		General routine	
Fruges	" 2		General routine	
Fruges	" 3		General routine	A/
Fruges	" 4		General routine	
Fruges	" 5		General routine	
Fruges	" 6		Digging urinal pit, grease trap & soakage pit, and replacing Incinerator for 59 Coy A.S.C.	
Fruges	" 7		Fodor lorry R.A.M.C. Ass: an - Engge to disinfect blankets &c for 2nd Life Gds 202 whilst disinfected for 2nd L Gds & 15 b for 7 of Machine Gun Sqdn. Lorry journey to Fodor to disinfect with coal & chloride Grease.	M/

No. 12 Section, 2nd Low: Sur: Co: R.A.M.C. T.F.   Army Form C. 2118.

WAR DIARY
or
INTELLIGENCE SUMMARY.
(Erase heading not required.)

Instructions regarding War Diaries and Intelligence Summaries are contained in F. S. Regs., Part II. and the Staff Manual respectively. Title pages will be prepared in manuscript.

Place	Date	Hour	Summary of Events and Information	Remarks and references to Appendices
Bruges	1916 Sept 8		General routine.	
Aire en Gohy	"		Today Disinfect. disinfecting 30 articles for 7th C.F.A. and 168 for and 214 for 3rd Field Squadron.	
Bruges	"	9	General routine	
Ruitsmond	"		Disinfecting 282 articles for No. 6 C.F.A.	M
Bruges	"	10	General routine.	
Bruges to Guiskart	"	11	Move	
Guiskart to Bellevine - Lompré	"	12	Move & afternoon, digging latrines for Officers Mess.	
Bulloy	Sept 13		General routine.	M

No 12 Section 2nd Louisian: W. Ram: I.F.   Army Form C. 2118.

WAR DIARY
or
INTELLIGENCE SUMMARY.
(Erase heading not required.)

Instructions regarding War Diaries and Intelligence
Summaries are contained in F. S. Regs., Part II.
and the Staff Manual respectively. Title pages
will be prepared in manuscript.

Place	Date	Hour	Summary of Events and Information	Remarks and references to Appendices
Bellevue Farm to Daours	1916 Sept 15		Move.	
Daours	"	16	General routine.	AF
Daours	"	16	Filling in holes in road by church.	AF
Daours	"	17	Removing refuse from rear of Officers mess	AF
Daours	"	18	Building incinerator at Officers mess, also burning refuse in yard	AF

No. 12 Section 2nd London Company R.A.M.C.

WAR DIARY
or
INTELLIGENCE SUMMARY.

Army Form C. 2118.

(Erase heading not required.)

Place	Date	Hour	Summary of Events and Information	Remarks and references to Appendices
Darcus	Sept 1916 19		Bath parade at Corbe	
Darcus	"	20	General routine.	
Darcus	"	21	General routine. Tested all water supplies for Brigade but had no time klebel Wasser.	
Darcus Le Quesnoy	"	22	ymove	
Le Quesnoy Fosseux le Mesnil	"	23	ymove	

Sanitary Section — Third Cavalry Div.

No. 12 Section 9th London Sanitary Co. RAMC T.F. **WAR DIARY** or **INTELLIGENCE SUMMARY**

Army Form C. 2118.

[Stamp: SANITARY SECTION — THIRD CAVALRY DIV.]

Place	Date	Hour	Summary of Events and Information	Remarks and references to Appendices
Trekenlegrand Guignup	1916 Sept 24	2 pm noe		
Guignup	" 25		Digging for latrines, setting well water pr Guignup Chapelle, making trough for gentle latrine, repairing of pump. Water supply of H.Q. château condemned.	MT
Guignup	" 26		Making incinerators for H.Q. division. 1 man sick in field 3rd Field Squadron	
Guignup	" 27		3 sacks coal sent out to Foden, 1 ston of coal brought back from Frerges. Disinfection of 1st Royal Dragoons bypren	MT

No. 12 Sec 2nd London Sanitary Coy (ATMCTF)

WAR DIARY
or
INTELLIGENCE SUMMARY.
(Erase heading not required.)

Army Form C. 2118.

Place	Date	Hour	Summary of Events and Information	Remarks and references to Appendices
Guigny	Sept 28		Incinerator for A.S.C. coal sent out to Foden. Disinfection of Intrepid dragoons completed.	MT
Guigny	" 29		Refuse pit. General sanitation. } 3rd Dragoon Guards disinfected	
Guigny	" 30		General routine. The 16 NCOs entered unapproving of the sanitary arrangements of the units to which they are attached.	MT

M.W. Turnton Capt.
30.9.16

140/188

3rd [ ]: Division

No. 12 Sanitary Section

Oct 1916

COMMITTEE FOR THE
MEDICAL HISTORY OF THE WAR
Date -2 DEC. 1916

Vol 21

War Diary
of
No 12 Sanitary Section
October 1916

N° 12 Section 9th London Sanitary Co. RAMC T.F. WAR DIARY or INTELLIGENCE SUMMARY.

Army Form C. 2118.

Instructions regarding War Diaries and Intelligence Summaries are contained in F. S. Regs., Part II. and the Staff Manual respectively. Title pages will be prepared in manuscript.

(Erase heading not required.)

Place	Date	Hour	Summary of Events and Information	Remarks and references to Appendices
Guigny	Octr 1st		General routine. Disinfection of 3rd Dragoon Guards completed.	
Guigny to Capelle	" 2	"	Move. Disinfection of "C" Machine Gun Squadron begun & completed.	M
Capelle	" 3	"	Lorry to Frugers for 1½ tn coal. Testing well water at Capelle. Bgde HQ. Police & Signal Troop disinfected.	
Capelle	" 4	"	Lorry to Foden disinfector, with 1½ tn coal. 6th Cavalry Field Amb'. disinfected. General routine. Investigation of attack of diphtheria among civil population of town. All swabs taken reported negative.	M

No. 18 Section, 9th London Sanitary Co. RAMC WAR DIARY or INTELLIGENCE SUMMARY.

Army Form C. 2118.

Place	Date	Hour	Summary of Events and Information	Remarks and references to Appendices
Capelle	Oct 5th	5—	Arrival of reinforcement. "E" Battery RHA 12.47 - at RHQ SWB e.13. General routine disinfection	NF
Capelle	" 6th	6—	Pte Fenning & Sharp appointed act LCpl (without pay) to attend RHQ Sharp as 6th Machine Gun Squadron. " Fenning " 1 " " " " " Stoker " 8 " " " " Making articles (sand) for making wells. Disinfection of North Somerset Yeomanry begun. Increasing rates received.	NF
Capelle	" 7"		Disinfection of Green Yeomanry by the Clayton machine at Pardin. General routine. Disinfection of North Somerset Yeomanry completed.	NF

No. 17 Section 9th Cavalry Sanitary Co.
Ranger

WAR DIARY
or
INTELLIGENCE SUMMARY.

Army Form C. 2118.

(Erase heading not required.)

Place	Date	Hour	Summary of Events and Information	Remarks and references to Appendices
	1916.			
Capelle	Octr. 8		Making active boards. General routine.	
Capelle	" 9		Rooney to Fruges. Disinfection of 84 C.F.A.	
Capelle	" 10		Party 16 todden disinfecter with pump, motor lorries to and spread 8th Cavalry Field Amb. HQrs. 8th Cavalry Brigade. General routine. "G" Battery disinfected.	M
Capelle	" 11		Lorry to Hesdin to take todden disinfecter. Sample taken from 2 civilian diphtheria case at Bimieux. General routine.	
			Disinfection of Royal Horse Guards commenced.	M

No 1 & 2 Section 3rd Cavalry Sanitary Corps

WAR DIARY
or
INTELLIGENCE SUMMARY.

Army Form C. 2118.

(Erase heading not required.)

Place	Date	Hour	Summary of Events and Information	Remarks and references to Appendices
	1916			
Capelle	Octr 12th		General routine. Disinfection of Royal Horse Guards completed. Sent officer taken yesterday at Brimeux reported position. General routine. Kerry to therein for repairs.	MF
Capelle	"	13th		
Capelle	"	14th	Wood from therein for making outric boxes. Disinfection of 10th Royal Hussars begun.	
Capelle	"	15th	General routine. Making outric boxes. Disinfection of 10th Royal Hussars completed. 8th Machine Gun Squadron disinfected.	
Capelle	"	16th	Returnies on leave. (16. 22.) Lorry back from therein.	
Capelle	"	17th	Two men came of diphtheria at Brimeux but no connection found except all men slept in same hut. Lorry on. Machine Gun Section Coaches. Lorry to therein for coal, and thence to Foden disinfector.	MF

No. 12 Section 2. London Sanitary Co
RUMMETZ
Army Form C. 2118.

WAR DIARY
or
INTELLIGENCE SUMMARY.

(Erase heading not required.)

Instructions regarding War Diaries and Intelligence Summaries are contained in F. S. Regs., Part II. and the Staff Manual respectively. Title pages will be prepared in manuscript.

Place	Date	Hour	Summary of Events and Information	Remarks and references to Appendices
	1916			
Capelle	Oct. 19th		General routine	
Beauxville			Pte Hayden returned, 9 run 1/c of horses. 4th Cavalry Field Amb' disinfected & completed our fumigation in the B.H.C., it had no connection with Rennery.	
Capelle to Bois-Jean	" "	19.20	Move	
Bois-Jean	" "	"	Off Head fixing Officer cook house at Chateau. Disinfection of 1st Life Guards commenced.	NF
Bois-Jean	" "	20th	Lorry to Hesdin for 15th coal, & to Capelle. Off Head at Chateau	
			General routine Disinfection of 1st Life Guards completed.	
Bois-Jean	" "	21st	General routine Disinfection of Leicesters (Yeomanry) begun. Two more civilian cases of diphtheria at Rennery. Owing to the mobility of inhabiting and of being unconnected with the divison, the travel cannot be prevented, and no action could be connected to, but trained orderly travels to all troops to be evacuated from it.	NF

No. 19 Section 2/1 London Sanitary Company
Rations

WAR DIARY
or
INTELLIGENCE SUMMARY.

Army Form C. 2118.

(Erase heading not required.)

Instructions regarding War Diaries and Intelligence Summaries are contained in F.S. Regs., Part II. and the Staff Manual respectively. Title pages will be prepared in manuscript.

Place	Date	Hour	Summary of Events and Information	Remarks and references to Appendices
	1916			
Bois-jean (Cottes)	22nd		General routine. Disinfection of incinerators & urinals completed.	
Bois-jean	23rd		Lorry to Etaples & Inclinent Plage. Water testing at Wailly.	MP
			General routine. 4th Machine Gun Squadron disinfected. Examined drainage system of 6th Brigade D.A.S. & Machined Pegs. Water testing at Wailly.	
Bois-jean	24th		Lorry to Wailly for Wood. "C" Squadron 2nd Life Guards disinfected. "B" Cavalry Field Amb. and HQrs 1st Life Guards disinfected.	
Bois-jean	25th		Lorry to Fruges with 5 cwt coal to Oxford grease. Split main finished for A.D.M.S.	
Bois-jean	26th		Disinfection of 1st Life Guards completed. Foden disinfector returned to unit. Sanitary arrangements for Div Canteen at Wailly put in place.	MT

T2134. Wt. W708–776. 500/000. 4/15. St J.C.&S.

No 19 Section 2nd Horse Sanitary Co. R.A.M.C. T.F.

WAR DIARY or INTELLIGENCE SUMMARY.

Army Form C. 2118.

Place	Date	Hour	Summary of Events and Information	Remarks and references to Appendices
	1916			
Bois-Jean	Oct 27th		Lorry to Beaurainville. General routine.	
Bois-Jean Maninal	" 28th		General routine. Inspected N.S. Yeomanry billets etc.	
Bois-Jean	" 29th		General routine	N.T.
Bois-Jean Camp	" 30th		General routine. Reported outbreak of diphtheria among civilians. Took mids of all child ensabling mosquito	
Bois-Jean	" 31st		Sanitary arrangements for Bois' Auxin or Vaulli improved. General routine.	N.T.
			The N.C.Os continued their work in improving the sanitation of the units to which they are attached.	

M.L. Thompson Capt.
2/c No 19 Sanitary Section

12 Sanitary Se
Vol 23

W返
Original
copy
Dec - 1916

SANITARY SECTION
THIRD CAVALRY DIV

Sanitary Section 1 Anderson Ca
Cavalry TF

WAR DIARY
or
INTELLIGENCE SUMMARY.

Army Form C. 2118.

Place	Date	Hour	Summary of Events and Information	Remarks and references to Appendices
Boisjean St Ome	1916 Dec	31st	General routine. Disinfecting at Essex Yeomanry. N.C.Os distributed thro division continued supervision sanitation	AT.

A.G.G. Thompson
Capt.
31.12.16

WAR DIARY or INTELLIGENCE SUMMARY

Army Form C. 2118.

(Stamp: SANITARY SECTION — THIRD CAVALRY DIV.)

Place	Date	Hour	Summary of Events and Information	Remarks and references to Appendices
	1916			
Bonleau See	27		Disinfection at 2nd Machine gun Squadron. Conducted Dis aly on Desert with 60 cwft. pulled tin for St Georges, Op	MT
Proceed Bouin & no Manaine			Saw the sick.	
Boiseau	"	28	Examined cases of mumps, Officers of 3rd Dragoon Gds. Park, disinfecting horses. R.T. refied. Down to Ruis a Lee with 30 cwft. petrol tin for Ammul Column.	MT
Beck. St Jans			Arranged for an of ridings cart, also for payment of any horse stained. Inspector cases of civilian diphtheria.	
Boisjean	"	29	General routine. Disinfecting Commencent at Royal Horse Guards. Inspection of the horse reported in civilian. None found.	MT
Machicoul				
Boisjean	"	30	Early to Fockart - Avion SP/Reap with eval. General routine. Inspected cases of civilian diphtheria.	MT
Crispy				MT

Army Form C. 2118.

WAR DIARY
or
INTELLIGENCE SUMMARY.

(Erase heading not required.)

Place	Date	Hour	Summary of Events and Information	Remarks and references to Appendices
	1916			
Boisjean	Dec 1st		Fixing sanitary arrangements for bivi School,	
Boisjean	"	2nd	Building incinerator for Officers mess.	M.T.
St Tom			Examined cases of diphtheria among civil population.	
Boisjean	"	3rd	Disinfecting at "C" Battery.	
			General routine.	
Boisjean	"	4th	General routine.	
			Repairing zinc baths.	
Boisjean	"	5th	152 cmplts felt chin through [?] pour [?]	
Boisjean	"	6th	Constructing incinerator for village.	M

Army Form C. 2118.

WAR DIARY
or
INTELLIGENCE SUMMARY.
(Erase heading not required.)

18th Sanitary Section 3rd Cavalry Co [Signature]

Instructions regarding War Diaries and Intelligence Summaries are contained in F. S. Regs., Part II. and the Staff Manual respectively. Title pages will be prepared in manuscript.

[Stamp: SANITARY SECTION THIRD CAVALRY DIV.]

Place	Date	Hour	Summary of Events and Information	Remarks and references to Appendices
	1916			
Boisjean Bert Plage	Dec 7th		General routine. Obtained trolies to empty the proves formed at Nedient Plage	MT
Boisjean Nedient Plage	"	8th	General routine. Inspected the village sanitation etc.	
Boisjean	"	9th	General routine.	MT
Boisjean	"	10th	General routine.	
Boisjean Conie St. Notin	"	11th	General routine. Cases of need from every civilian population inspected.	AT

T2134. Wt. W708—776. 500000. 4/15. Sir J. C. & S.

Army Form C. 2118.

WAR DIARY
or
INTELLIGENCE SUMMARY.
(Erase heading not required.)

Instructions regarding War Diaries and Intelligence Summaries are contained in F.S. Regs., Part II. and the Staff Manual respectively. Title pages will be prepared in manuscript.

[Stamp: SANITARY SECTION / THIRD CAVALRY DIV.]

Place	Date	Hour	Summary of Events and Information	Remarks and references to Appendices
	1916			
Bonjean Medical Rep.	Dec 12th		General routine. Proceeded to intelligence at noon to the 6th Brigade Staff Captain.	MT
Bonjean "	13th		General routine.	
Bonjean "	14th		Lorry journey 15 hundredweight to supply petrol this session. Taken to the lines at Plage.	MT
Bonjean Medical Rep.	15th		General routine. Lecture given at divisional school on sanitation.	MT
Bonjean "	16th		Lorry journey to St Jans with 58 petrol tins for 1st Royal Dragoons.	MT

No 91 **Headquarters 3rd Cavalry Brigade** Bennett

Army Form C. 2118.

WAR DIARY
or
INTELLIGENCE SUMMARY.

(Erase heading not required.)

Instructions regarding War Diaries and Intelligence Summaries are contained in F. S. Regs., Part II. and the Staff Manual respectively. Title pages will be prepared in manuscript.

[Stamp: SANITARY SECTION * THIRD CAVALRY DIV.]

Place	Date	Hour	Summary of Events and Information	Remarks and references to Appendices
	1916			
Boinjeau Wailly	Dec 17th		General routine. Inspected machine gun gallop after the divisional headquarters held mid.	M.
Boinjeau	" 18th		General routine.	M.
Boinjeau	" 19th		General routine.	M.
Boinjeau	" 20th		Fixing sanitary arrangements for Div'l Cavalier at Trephiel.	M.
Boinjeau Beumetz	" 21st		General routine. Saw siding of the Ammunition column.	M.

No. 12 Veterinary Ambulance Co. Army Form C. 2118.

WAR DIARY
or
INTELLIGENCE SUMMARY.

(Erase heading not required.)

SANITARY SECTION *THIRD CAVALRY DIV.*

Place	Date	Hour	Summary of Events and Information	Remarks and references to Appendices
	1916			
Boisjean	Dec 22nd		General routine	
Boisjean Compiègne dist.	"	23rd	General routine. Saw the sick of the ammunition park	M.
Boisjean	"	24th	General routine.	M.
Boisjean	"	25th	General routine.	M.
Boisjean Bernard Buir du me.	"	26th	General routine. Saw the sick of G.Battery and the ammunition column.	M.

140/1900

3rd Cav. Div.

No. 12 Sanitary Section

Dec. 1916

COMMITTEE FOR THE
MEDICAL HISTORY OF THE WAR
Date 31 JAN. 1917

12 Sanit Sec.
140/1846   Vol 22

War Diary
for the
Month of November 1916.

SANITARY SECTION
THIRD CAVALRY DIV.

COMMITTEE FOR THE
MEDICAL HISTORY OF THE WAR
Date -3 JAN. 1917

No 12 Section
2nd Lond San:
CO: Ramc.T.F.

Nov 1916

Army Form C. 2118.

The 12 Regiment of Hussars Comdg. C. Rouet — WAR DIARY or INTELLIGENCE SUMMARY.

Instructions regarding War Diaries and Intelligence Summaries are contained in F. S. Regs., Part II. and the Staff Manual respectively. Title pages will be prepared in manuscript.

(Erase heading not required.)

SANITARY SECTION
No.
Date
THIRD CAVALRY DIV.

Place	Date	Hour	Summary of Events and Information	Remarks and references to Appendices
	1916.			
Bois-Jean	Jan 1	1st	General routine.	
Nielwert Pap.			Inspected drainage system of O.R.S.	
Bois-Jean	"	2nd	General routine.	
Min. Ind.			Took records of existing recup. system in Royal Horse Guards.	M.5
Bois-Jean	"	3rd	Lorry to Hucheuvre Plage & for material for latrines.	
			General routine.	
Torcy	"		Examined inspected camp of C.S.M. in Nissen wagons.	
Bois-Jean	"	4th	Lorry to Eeden disinfector with 6 cwt P. coal.	
Bois-Jean	"	5th	General routine.	
Bois-Jean	"	6th	Fixing shelter for latrine at Canteen Waille.	
			Lorry to Hucheuvre Plage with one box disinfector for O.C. C.F.A.	M.7

WAR DIARY
or
INTELLIGENCE SUMMARY.

Army Form C. 2118.

Place	Date	Hour	Summary of Events and Information	Remarks and references to Appendices
	1916			
Bois-jean	Nov 7		Lieut J.S. Develin (Retain) arrived to France with 1 Box Disinfector for 9th C.F.A.	
Medical Dep Boisjean	"	8th	Received reported and given medals in O.R.S. Men attached to 8 Divisional Cav. Car Scho Today + been returned to Section.	AT
Bois-jean	"	9th	General routine.	
Bois-jean	"	10th	General routine.	
Bois-jean	"	11th	25 Relief tins sent to to in Schol. General routine.	AT

Army Form C. 2118

WAR DIARY
or
INTELLIGENCE SUMMARY.

No. 19 Section 2 Foster Sanitaire
R.C.M.C.T.

(Erase heading not required.)

Instructions regarding War Diaries and Intelligence Summaries are contained in F. S. Regs., Part II. and the Staff Manual respectively. Title pages will be prepared in manuscript.

SANITARY SECTION
No.
Date
THIRD CAVALRY DIV.

Place	Date	Hour	Summary of Events and Information	Remarks and references to Appendices
	1916.			
Bois-jean	Nov 12th		General routine.	
Bois-jean	" 13th		General routine.	AG
Bois-jean	" 14th		Headqr. 1st Royals disinfected. General routine.	
Bois-jean	" 15		General routine.	AG
Bois-jean	" 16th		General routine.	

Army Form C. 2118

WAR DIARY
or
INTELLIGENCE SUMMARY.

No. 12 Section 9th Sanitary Co.
J. Rawcliff

(Erase heading not required.)

Instructions regarding War Diaries and Intelligence Summaries are contained in F. S. Regs., Part II. and the Staff Manual respectively. Title pages will be prepared in manuscript.

SANITARY SECTION
THIRD CAVALRY DIV.

Place	Date	Hour	Summary of Events and Information	Remarks and references to Appendices
Bois-jean	Nov. 1916 17th		Making 2 incinerators at Wailly. General routine.	
Bois-jean	"	18th	Testing well water at Wailly	AB
Bois-jean	"	19th	General routine.	
Bois-jean	"	20th	General routine.	
Bois-jean	"	21	Later testing at Courcelles le Petit. General routine.	AB

WAR DIARY or INTELLIGENCE SUMMARY.

Army Form C. 2118

N⁰ 12 Section, North Sanitary Co.
Rawlett

Place	Date	Hour	Summary of Events and Information	Remarks and references to Appendices
Bois jean	1916 Nov 22ᵈ		General routine	
Bois jean	" 23		Lorry journey to 3rd Dragoon Gds & North Somerset Yeomanry with 50 hrs for each regiment.	M
Bois jean	" 24		General routine	
Bois jean	" 25		Lorry journey to 10th Rd Hussars with 50 latrine hrs.	
Bois jean	" 26		Lorry journey to 9th N.Y. Sg (offrs) Leinster Yeo (Sregd) (Royal 2nd Lifegds) and 1st Life Gds (Sreusin) with 50 latrine hrs for each unit. Constructing sink for Officers' Mess.	M
Bois jean	" 27		General routine.	

Army Form C. 2118.

WAR DIARY
or
INTELLIGENCE SUMMARY.
(Erase heading not required.)

Instructions regarding War Diaries and Intelligence Summaries are contained in F. S. Regs., Part II. and the Staff Manual respectively. Title pages will be prepared in manuscript.

SANITARY SECTION
No.
Date
THIRD CAVALRY DIV.

Place	Date	Hour	Summary of Events and Information	Remarks and references to Appendices
Bois Jean	Nov 28		Constructing incinerator for Divisional School. Making & fixing protector for reflector over lamp in A.D.M.S. office.	AT
Bois Jean	" 29		Lorry journey to Aire-en-Lis and (Rodelols) with 30 latrine bins. Making urinal & urinal troughs for Divl. School.	AT
Bois Jean	" 30		General routine. Making latrine seat 9c for Divisional School.	

A.W. Thornton Capt.
O.C No 12 Section, 2nd Lowland San. Co.
Bons. S.J.

140/1917 Vol 24

3rd Lon. Div.

War Diary of

No. 12 Sanitary Section.

2nd London Sanitary Company

R.A.M.C. T.F

For January 1917

COMMITTEE FOR THE
MEDICAL HISTORY OF THE WAR.
Date 13 MAR. 1917

Army Form C. 2118.

WAR DIARY
or
INTELLIGENCE SUMMARY.
(Erase heading not required.)

Instructions regarding War Diaries and Intelligence Summaries are contained in F.S. Regs., Part II. and the Staff Manual respectively. Title pages will be prepared in manuscript.

SANITARY SECTION
THIRD CAVALRY DIV.

Place	Date	Hour	Summary of Events and Information	Remarks and references to Appendices
Bois Jean St Josse	1-1-17		General Routine. Foden Steam Disinfector with "B" Squadron, Essex Yeomanry for disinfecting duties.	
Bois Jean Aubin-st-Plage	2-1-17		General Routine. Disinfector with "B" & "C" Squadrons, 10th Royal Hussars for disinfecting duties.	
Crépay	"		Inspection of civilian disinfection cases reported by French Mission.	
Bois Jean	"		Two S.R. on lorry to Sapien. Preparation for evacuation of field billets.	
Aubin-st-Plage	"		Disinfector with 10th Royal Hussars for disinfectory duties. Lecture at Divisional school.	
Bois Jean Aubin-st-Plage	4-1-17		Two S.R. on lorry with Steam coal to Sapien. Disinfector with 8th Cavalry Field Ambulance for disinfecting duties.	
Bois Jean Complies no Sommes	5-1-17		Evacuation of Bois Jean - lorry with stores etc. to new billets Sapien. Disinfector with "A" Squadron Royal Horse Guards - disinfecting duties.	

Army Form C. 2118.

WAR DIARY
or
INTELLIGENCE SUMMARY.
(Erase heading not required.)

Instructions regarding War Diaries and Intelligence Summaries are contained in F. S. Regs., Part II. and the Staff Manual respectively. Title pages will be prepared in manuscript.

SANITARY SECTION
THIRD CAVALRY DIV.

Place	Date	Hour	Summary of Events and Information	Remarks and references to Appendices
Inspua	6-1-17		Lorry to Roisnest with coal for Loden, on return journey picking up remainder of stores at Bois Jean.	
Roisnest	"		Disinfector with "G" Battery Royal Horse Artillery. Disinfector returned to Inspua.	M7
Rest. Inspua	7-1-17		Further arrangements made tempty form at Medical Reg. General routine	M7
Inspua	8-1-17		General routine.	
Inspua Hemore	9-1-17		General routine. Disinfector went to 6th Cavalry Field Ambulance.	
Inspua	10-1-17		Lorry to Hemore with coal for Loden. General routine	
Enger			More diphtheria cases reported. Now proved the genuine article.	M7

T2134. Wt. W708—776. 500000. 4/15. Sir J. C. & S.

Army Form C. 2118.

WAR DIARY
or
INTELLIGENCE SUMMARY.
(Erase heading not required.)

Instructions regarding War Diaries and Intelligence Summaries are contained in F. S. Regs., Part II. and the Staff Manual respectively. Title pages will be prepared in manuscript.

SANITARY SECTION
THIRD CAVALRY DIV'N

Place	Date	Hour	Summary of Events and Information	Remarks and references to Appendices
Inforid	11-1-19		General routine	
Aix en Issart	"		Disinfector with "C" Squadron 3rd Dragoon Guards.	
Inforid	12-1-19		General routine & car tipped on enormous brooks	ND
Aix en Issart	"		Disinfector with "C" Squadron 3rd Dragoon Guards.	
Inforid	13-1-19		General routine	
Aix en Issart	"		Disinfector with "A" Squadron, 3rd Dragoon Guards	ND
Inforid	14-1-19		Arrival of 1 CPL reinforcements from base. See 2nd Cav. Div. Diary with 9 tubs & 81st Co. A.S.C. Energy.	
Marquise	"		Disinfector with "B" Squad. & Headquarters, 3rd Dragon Guards.	ND
Inforid	15-1-19		Disinfector to Supply Column Matingles, Marcheleur Estaires.	
"	"		General routine	

Army Form C. 2118.

WAR DIARY
or
INTELLIGENCE SUMMARY.
(Erase heading not required.)

Instructions regarding War Diaries and Intelligence Summaries are contained in F. S. Regs., Part II. and the Staff Manual respectively. Title pages will be prepared in manuscript.

[Stamp: SANITARY SECTION * THIRD CAVALRY DIV'N * No. Date]

Place	Date	Hour	Summary of Events and Information	Remarks and references to Appendices
Tripoli	16-1-19		General routine.	
Medinat el Reys			Motor cast struck.	
Tripoli	17-1-19		Lorry to Hoosh with coal for stoves.	NP
Tripoli	18-1-19		Stoves returned to Mark from workshops.	
			General routine.	
Tripoli	19-1-19		General routine.	
Rafat Puits Remalt			Arranged for disinfection of prisoners camp and 2nd Field Squadron R.E.	NP
Tripoli	20-1-19		108 increased dose Dis. Hypt, suspense concealer of heminator.	
			General routine.	
Medinat el Reys			Instructs M.O.M.S. tres Scalin hospital.	
Tripoli	21-1-19		Transfector proceeded to Mescavator, North Covered Economy.	NP
			Officer for duty.	
			General routine.	
Puits Remalt			Selected site for spray baths.	

WAR DIARY
or
INTELLIGENCE–SUMMARY.
(Erase heading not required.)

Army Form C. 2118.

Instructions regarding War Diaries and Intelligence Summaries are contained in F. S. Regs., Part II. and the Staff Manual respectively. Title pages will be prepared in manuscript.

Place	Date	Hour	Summary of Events and Information	Remarks and references to Appendices
Infied	22-1-17		Party to Supply Column Mickelelys for inspection. General routine.	
Forges, Infied	23-1-17		Inspected sanitation of D.A.S. and 2nd lift grenades. General routine. Inspector returned to Mickelelys to report re burst steam pipe.	M
Infied	24-1-17		General routine	
Infied	25-1-17		General routine	
St Jean Infied	26-1-17		Inspected sanitation of Essex yeomanry. General routine. Inspected sanitation of 10th Hussars	M
Maisuil Infied	27-1-17		Party proceeded to R.E. Montreuil, to pick up spray bath and conveyed same to 3rd Field Squadron to Fort Brimeule. General routine.	
Aubin S:Vaast			Case of diphtheria reported, man a nurses of C. B. Wholewhid at St Johnburg ?	M

WAR DIARY
or
INTELLIGENCE SUMMARY.
(Erase heading not required.)

Army Form C. 2118.

Instructions regarding War Diaries and Intelligence Summaries are contained in F. S. Regs., Part II. and the Staff Manual respectively. Title pages will be prepared in manuscript.

SANITARY SECTION
THIRD CAVALRY DIV.

Place	Date	Hour	Summary of Events and Information	Remarks and references to Appendices
Insped	28.1.19		General routine.	
			Foster disinfector proving badly & all disinfection stopped.	MT
Insped	29.1.19		General routine.	
Beaurainville Hqrs. en route			Inspected Supply & Ammunition. Inspected station of 3rd Dragoon Guards.	
Insped	30.1.19		Foster returned to Workshops, Beaurainville - Owing to the constant breakdowns it has been found advisable to return Disinfector, than there is no workshops here to do ours - or - toward with 60 petrol tins for sanitary purposes to 3rd Dragoon Guards.	MT
			Heavy to Workshops Beaurainville and sent real for Disinfector, then there is no workshops here to do ours - or - toward with 60 petrol tins for sanitary purposes to 3rd Dragoon Guards.	
Enquin Insped	31.1.19		Two cases of diptheria reported by French transport authorities. General routine	MT
			During the month 16 N.C.O.'s men attached to the various regiments of the Division continued their work of supervising the general sanitary condition of the areas occupied by the division.	

M.W.Thompson
Capt. R.A.M.C
O/C No 12 Sanitary Section
attached. 3rd Cav.l. Div.

WAR DIARY

OF No 12 SANITARY SECTION

2nd LONDON SANITARY COMPANY
R.A.M.C. T.F.

FOR

JANUARY
1917

War Diary of

No. 12 Sanitary Section.

2ⁿᵈ London Sanitary Company RAMC.T.F.

February 1917

140/204 3.

COMMITTEE FOR THE
MEDICAL HISTORY OF THE WAR
Date 11 MAY.1917

Army Form C. 2118.

WAR DIARY
of
INTELLIGENCE SUMMARY.
(Erase heading not required.)

Instructions regarding War Diaries and Intelligence Summaries are contained in F. S. Regs., Part II. and the Staff Manual respectively. Title pages will be prepared in manuscript.

[Stamp: SANITARY SECTION, THIRD CAVALRY DIV.]

Place	Date	Hour	Summary of Events and Information	Remarks and references to Appendices
Lapied	1-2-19		General Routine	
"	2-2-19		General routine	M.
"	3-2-19		General routine	
Beauraville	4-2-19		Examined camp marks in the Supply Column	
Tupied	5-2-19		General routine	M.
"	6-2-19		General routine. Place to check emptying of latrines.	
"	7-2-19		General routine	M.

T2134. Wt. W708—776. 50/000. 4/15. Sir J. C. & S.

Army Form C. 2118.

WAR DIARY
or
INTELLIGENCE SUMMARY.
(Erase heading not required.)

Instructions regarding War Diaries and Intelligence Summaries are contained in F. S. Regs., Part II. and the Staff Manual respectively. Title pages will be prepared in manuscript.

[Stamp: SANITARY SECTION * THIRD CAVALRY DIV *]

Place	Date	Hour	Summary of Events and Information	Remarks and references to Appendices
Infield	8-2-17		General routine	
Engagte. Trefnud.	9-2-17		Inspluit sanitation of R.H.Guards, K.Bullog. Ammunition Column. Lorry to Supply Column Montrelpo, Beauvencelle, for fortnightly inspection — General routine	M.T.
"	10.2.17		Return of lorry from coptelpo. General routine	
"	11.2.17		General routine	
"	12.2.17		General routine. Two O.R. men reported for duty (attached)	M.T.
"	13.2.17		General routine. Lorry to Div. Headquarters conveying back	
"	14.2.17		General routine	M.

Army Form C. 2118.

WAR DIARY
or
INTELLIGENCE SUMMARY.
(Erase heading not required.)

Instructions regarding War Diaries and Intelligence Summaries are contained in F. S. Regs., Part II. and the Staff Manual respectively. Title pages will be prepared in manuscript.

Place	Date	Hour	Summary of Events and Information	Remarks and references to Appendices
Infeed	15.2.19		General routine	
"	16.2.19		Lorry to Plumpton with coal for three Inspectors. General routine	NT.
"	17.2.19		Your Arson Inspector attached to 1st Royal Dragoons for Inspecting duties (Plumpton). General routine	NT.
"	18.2.19		General routine. 1 N.C.O. to Denain Bn School for instruction	—
"	19.2.19		Lorry to Marcoing with coal to Denain Taken with 6th Machine Gun Squad for Inspecting duties General routine.	NT.

T2134. Wt. W708—776. 500000. 4/15. Sir J. C. & S.

WAR DIARY
or
INTELLIGENCE SUMMARY.

(Erase heading not required.)

Army Form C. 2118.

Instructions regarding War Diaries and Intelligence Summaries are contained in F. S. Regs., Part II. and the Staff Manual respectively. Title pages will be prepared in manuscript.

Place	Date	Hour	Summary of Events and Information	Remarks and references to Appendices
Tupied	20.2.17		Gower said Demanded Ammunition Column. Remitly for disinfecting duties — General routine	
"	21.2.17		General routine — 103 P.B. men reported for duty (attached). Shewing up sanitary arrangements at billets in Tupied area.	AT.
"	22.2.17		General routine.	
"	23.2.17		General routine. Paid for inspecting camps at Richard Pays. General routine and upon leaving.	AT.
Rechi. Tupied.	24.2.17			
"	25.2.17		Disinfection of billets (measles). General routine.	AT.

WAR DIARY
or
INTELLIGENCE SUMMARY.
(Erase heading not required.)

Army Form C. 2118.

Instructions regarding War Diaries and Intelligence Summaries are contained in F. S. Regs., Part II. and the Staff Manual respectively. Title pages will be prepared in manuscript.

Place	Date	Hour	Summary of Events and Information	Remarks and references to Appendices
Tréport	26.2.19		General routine.	
St Jans	27.2.19		Inspected Sanitation of 6th L.F.G. Guards	MF
Tréport			General routine	
Rouen			Arranged programme for disinfectors which has been hung up owing to the condition of the roads	MF
Tréport	28.2.19		Lorry to St Paul's Barracks arrived and sent for horses, pushing up timber at Montreuil on return journey.	
			Inspected sanitation of divisional H.Q. & units attached.	MF
			During the month 15 N.C.O. and men, attached to the various Regiments of the Division continued their work of supervising the general sanitary conditions of the areas occupied by the units	

A. G. C. Thompson
Capt. RAMC.
Officer Commanding No 12 Sanitary Section
attached 3rd Cavalry Division

War Diary of
No. 12 Sanitary Section
2nd London Sanitary Company R.A.M.C.,T.F

February 1917

WAR DIARY of 3rd Cav. Div.

No. 12 SANITARY SECTION of the

2nd LONDON SANITARY Co

R.A.M.C.T

MARCH 1917

40/2067

Vol 26

COMMITTEE FOR THE
MEDICAL HISTORY OF THE WAR
Date — 6 JUN.1917

WAR DIARY or INTELLIGENCE SUMMARY.

Army Form C. 2118.

(Erase heading not required.)

Instructions regarding War Diaries and Intelligence Summaries are contained in F.S. Regs., Part II. and the Staff Manual respectively. Title pages will be prepared in manuscript.

[Stamp: SANITARY SECTION — THIRD CAVALRY DIV.]

Place	Date	Hour	Summary of Events and Information	Remarks and references to Appendices
	MARCH			
Inspred	1st		Making and stencilling 100 notice Boards for marking water supply	
Aire-a-hut Inspred les Puits Berrault	2nd		Examined suspected infection officer 3rd Dragoon Guards. German Box works. Completing notice Boards. Foden steam Disinfector with 3rd Field Squadron	M.S.
Inspred les Puits Berrault	3rd		General routine. Disinfector with 3rd Field Squadron	
Rosoy Inspred Compiegnieulle les Pierce	4th		Inspected manufacture of K. Battery. Saw completion reported by French Mission. N.V. dippans. General routine. Disinfector with Ammunition Park and Auxiliary Horse Transport	M.S.
Inspred	5th		General routine. Lorry with Steam coal for Foden disinfector to Compiegnieulle les Pierce.	
Medinal Cuvy			Inspected sanitation of Lieuts Germans.	M.S.

2353 Wt. W2544/1454. 700,000 5/15 D. D. & L. A.D.S.S./Forms/C. 2118.

Army Form C. 2118.

WAR DIARY
or
INTELLIGENCE SUMMARY.
(Erase heading not required.)

Instructions regarding War Diaries and Intelligence Summaries are contained in F. S. Regs., Part II. and the Staff Manual respectively. Title pages will be prepared in manuscript.

Place	Date	Hour	Summary of Events and Information	Remarks and references to Appendices
	MARCH			
Lupsee	6th		General routine.	
Verton			Inspected sanitation of 2nd Life Guards.	A.T.
Inspected	7th		General routine.	
Bois Jean			Lorry to Verton with empty petrol tins for 2nd Life Guards.	
Inspected	8th		Inspected 7th Machine Gun Squadron	A.T.
			General routine.	
St Denouval			Disinfector with Assc: Horse Transport.	
Campigneulles			Inspected sanitation of Ammunition Park.	
Les Petites	9th		General routine.	
Inspected			Lorry to Touvent workshops for fortnightly inspection	A.T.
Embry			Disinfector with "G" Bat. Royal Horse Artillery.	
Beauvoir	10th		Inspected sanitation of Supply Column.	A.T.
Inspected			General routine.	
Campagne			Disinfector with Somerset Supply Column.	

WAR DIARY
or
INTELLIGENCE SUMMARY.

(Erase heading not required.)

Army Form C. 2118.

Place	Date	Hour	Summary of Events and Information	Remarks and references to Appendices
	MARCH			
Inspied	11th		General routine.	
Beauvainville			Disinfector with Section 1, Divisional Supply Colm.	M.
Inspied	12th		General routine.	
Beauvainville			Disinfector with Section II and Headquarters, Divisional Supply Colm.	
Marles			Cases of men washed in a refugee train passing through this area.	
Inspied	13th		General routine.	
Acc-en-ient			Disinfector with 3rd Dragoon Guards B Squadron R.E.	OS.
"Puits Bunneth"			Hospital Sanitation of 3rd Field Squadron R.E.	
Inspied	14th		General routine.	
Acc-en-ient			Disinfector with 3rd Dragoon Guards.	
Manyed			Arranged disinfection of 6th Pioneer Battalion with reg. Captain Col. Ripsol.	OS.
Inspied	15th		General routine.	
Nadinal			Two cases of more measles in civilian population. Found two others and one whooping cough.	OS.

WAR DIARY
or
INTELLIGENCE SUMMARY.

(Erase heading not required)

Army Form C. 2118.

Instructions regarding War Diaries and Intelligence Summaries are contained in F.S. Regs., Part II. and the Staff Manual respectively. Title pages will be prepared in manuscript.

Place	Date	Hour	Summary of Events and Information	Remarks and references to Appendices
	MARCH			
Inspected	16th		General routine	
Aire-en-soissant			Disinfector with 3rd Dragoon Guards "A" & "B" Squadron	
Hinges & Maroeuil			Disinfector with 3rd Dragoon Guards "C" Squadron	
Oppin			Inspected ventilation of N.C.O. room/y.o. Conf. Read of fever outbreak at Beaurain station	MT
Inspected	17th		Disinfection of Billets 3rd Dragoon Guards	
			Disinfector with North Somerset Yeomanry & "a" Squadron & Headquarters	
Oppin				
Tropied			Conf. Re measures among the H.Q. divisional input troop.	MT
Inspected	18th		General routine	
Mont Bernenchon Plateau			Disinfector with North Somerset Yeomanry & "B" Squadron	
Inspected	19th		General routine	MT
			Lorry returned from Divisional workshops (thoroughly overhauled)	
Aubin St Vaast			Disinfected with 1st Royal Dragoons	
Aire a Mont			Saw the adjutant & M.O. of 3rd Dragoon Guards with Pvt. Meadows	MT

WAR DIARY
or
INTELLIGENCE SUMMARY.

Army Form C. 2118.

(Erase heading not required.)

Place	Date	Hour	Summary of Events and Information	Remarks and references to Appendices
	MARCH			
Infield	20th		General routine	
Phenomen			Disinfector with 1st Royal Dragoons "A" Squadron	
Furnes			Took men of suspected civilian diphtheria (children). We did not spot...	NT
Infield	21st		General routine	
Inecen			Lorry with steam gen. for lorries to Inecen	
			Disinfector with 5th Brigade Headquarters & Baron Fermency	NT
Infield	22nd		General routine	
Rinhoval			Disinfector with 10th Royal Hussars "A" Squadron	NT
Infield	23rd		General routine	
Schut Tourcop			Disinfector with 10th Royal Hussars "B" & "HQ" Squadron	
Venton			Case of civilian diphtheria reported by Frank Mission was undoubtedly measles.	NT
Infield	24th		General routine	
Crecy			Disinfector with 5th Machine Gun Squadron	NT

Army Form C. 2118.

WAR DIARY
or
INTELLIGENCE SUMMARY.
(Erase heading not required.)

Instructions regarding War Diaries and Intelligence Summaries are contained in F. S. Regs., Part II. and the Staff Manual respectively. Title pages will be prepared in manuscript.

Place	Date	Hour	Summary of Events and Information	Remarks and references to Appendices
	MARCH			
Ypres	25th		General routine	
Bruges			Disinfector with Royal Horse Guards Headquarters & "B" Squadron	MT
Ypres	26th		Lorry with steam sent to town to Bruges	
Hospital Kells			Disinfector with Royal Horse Guards "A" Squadron	MT
Ypres	27th		General routine	
Hospital Kemmel Ypres			Disinfector with "D" Squadron Royal Horse Guards & 1st Bartfield Ambulance	MT
St Omer.	28th		Acting Corpl CSM. (civilian) was found to be requiring room from JN.	
Ypres			General routine	MT
Campagnolle en Lavée			Disinfector returned to Headquarters from Bruges	
Ypres	29th		Inspected washing of 7th Corpul H.Q.	
			General routine	MT
Ypres	30th		Disinfector to ADS Headquarters for duty.	MT

WAR DIARY
or
INTELLIGENCE SUMMARY.

Army Form C. 2118.

(Erase heading not required.)

Instructions regarding War Diaries and Intelligence Summaries are contained in F. S. Regs., Part II. and the Staff Manual respectively. Title pages will be prepared in manuscript.

Place	Date	Hour	Summary of Events and Information	Remarks and references to Appendices
Infect Heemel Sanitary Section	31/24		General routine. Disinfector with 6th C.F.A. returned to Inspec. The Italian barrage have no latrines or any idea of hygiene however now under the Sanitary hyperi have completed their latrines. The Sanit Officer is charge permits to visit during the month 19 h.£06 men, attached to the various regiments of the Division were seen. Men were of informing the sanitary condition in the areas occupied by the unit. Summary of boilage, boat consumption e/c of articles disinfected during the month Mileage 160. Coal consumpt: 4,200 Kilos Articles disinfected 5,879. of which the great Majority was blankets.  M M Thompson Capt RAMC oc No12 Sanitary Section 3rd Cavalry Division	

War Diary of

No. 12 Sanitary Section of the
2nd London Sanitary Co.
RAMC T.

March 1917

April 1917.

140/2087

3rd Lond. Div.

War Diary for APRIL 1917.

No 12 Sanitary Section

2ND LONDON SANITARY Co. Ramc T.

Vol 27

COMMITTEE FOR THE
MEDICAL HISTORY OF THE WAR
Date −6 JUN. 1917

Army Form C. 2118.

WAR DIARY
or
INTELLIGENCE SUMMARY.
(Erase heading not required.)

Instructions regarding War Diaries and Intelligence Summaries are contained in F. S. Regs., Part II. and the Staff Manual respectively. Title pages will be prepared in manuscript.

Place	Date	Hour	Summary of Events and Information	Remarks and references to Appendices
TREPIED	APRIL 1		General routine	
TREPIED	" 2		General routine.	MT
TREPIED	" 3		Started lorry to Inneval Rest Station, Parkinent Plage. Picking up stores and blankets and conveying same to Boulogne. (two journeys)	MT
TREPIED	" 4		Lorry to SPRS Hesdment Plage, picking up 20 men and conveying them to Beauvainville, also taking stores from the unit and learns to Railhead Montreuil. Preparations for a forward move.	MT
TREPIED	" 5		Divisional move to Hondegrel.	MT
NIAGLIQUEL				

Army Form C. 2118.

WAR DIARY
or
INTELLIGENCE SUMMARY.
(Erase heading not required.)

Instructions regarding War Diaries and Intelligence Summaries are contained in F. S. Regs., Part II. and the Staff Manual respectively. Title pages will be prepared in manuscript.

Place	Date	Hour	Summary of Events and Information	Remarks and references to Appendices
MARQUEGLISE	April 6		General routine.	
MARQUEGLISE / MONCHEL	7th		Hd Qrs. moved from Marquegliese to Monchel.	AT
MONCHEL	8th		Hd Qrs moved from Monchel to Souez en Artois.	
GOUY-en-ARTOIS				AT
"	9		Four men sent to dressing stations from this unit to collect the names of wounded who might pass through. I joined the heavy section of 4 field ambulances so that the 4 M.S.C. drivers run up alone.	
"	10th		Waited for ambulances.	
ARRAS	11th		Moved with heavy section to Arras.	
GOUY-en-ARTOIS	12th		Moved back to Gouy. Placed myself in touch with O/C 25th Sanitary Section at Gouy.	AT
"	13th		Inspected camps occupied by this division in Gouy.	AT
"	14th		Arranged for delivering the slop for 8th Brigade. Sent lorry to Arras with 75 stretchers and stretchers a 60 gaits of pistol.	AT
"	15th		Stemilizing and other work done for O/C 25th Sanitary Section.	AT

2353 Wt. W2544/1454 750,000 5/15 D. D. & L.   A.D.S.S./Forms/C. 2118.

WAR DIARY
or
INTELLIGENCE SUMMARY.

(Erase heading not required.)

Army Form C. 2118.

Instructions regarding War Diaries and Intelligence Summaries are contained in F. S. Regs., Part II. and the Staff Manual respectively. Title pages will be prepared in manuscript.

Place	Date	Hour	Summary of Events and Information	Remarks and references to Appendices
Camp en Artois WAVANS	16th.		Moved back via Doullens to Wavans	AT.
"	17th.		Endeavoured to get in touch with O/C Sanitary Section of this area.	AT.
"	18th.		Corporal Hood left to join the R.E. Two men sent to Cav. Corps Depot, Remaisnil for duty.	AT.
"	19th.		Moved to Le petit Rocquigny.	AT.
Rocquigny	20th.			AT.
"	1st.		The two men detached on 9th returned from Marieux chateau.	AT.
"	2nd.		Baths were picked from divisional dumps & & repaired	AT.
"	3rd.		General Routine	AT.

WAR DIARY
or
INTELLIGENCE SUMMARY.
(Erase heading not required.)

Army Form C. 2118.

Place	Date	Hour	Summary of Events and Information	Remarks and references to Appendices
Acquipal	24th		General Routine.	
"	25th		General Routine.	
"	26th		General Routine.	
Hesdin Le Pinoy Mouquett	27th		Arranged for 170 well which brought the horses, with the C.R.E. C.O. & Corps Hoskin and the 2nd Field Squadron and want to get any wood. Inspected stagnation of the 1 Echiives. They have improved slightly.	AT.
Dompierre	28th		The 1st Life Guards having no watered are unable to do much to comply with the orgs explained, fly proof measures indicated on the G. H.Q. memorandum.	AT.
Wakincourt			3rd Field Squadron are in the same state, anxious to do anything if materials are supplied.	AT.
Vire-chaussy, Y Row, Grey			Ammunition column in the same predicament. 1st Royal Dragoons the same. Tested well for the C.R.Hqs. with horneton tap.	AT.

WAR DIARY
or
INTELLIGENCE SUMMARY.

Army Form C. 2118.

Place	Date	Hour	Summary of Events and Information	Remarks and references to Appendices
Avrinjul	29th		Extra troops billeted by coy from Herdin establd.	AT
Newpont			North Somerset Yeomanry had no urinals or trench latrines etc.	
Pt Prinx.			O.C. 3rd D. G. repairs to do anything about building arrangements until material is supplied.	AT
Avrinjul	30th		Ground Routine. The present area occupied by the division is roughly 17.6 square miles. Troops are in 37 villages. There is hardly a single latrine Coy mess pit or bucket left in the area. There are no latrine boards or walls and no material is being provided to provide built sanitary conveniences to replace those which have previously existed by the division who are leaving this area.	

McThornton Captn
RAMC
O/C Sanitary Section
Third Cavalry Div.

War Diary for April 1917

No. 12 Sanitary Section

2nd London Sanitary Co. R.A.M.C.T.

WAR DIARY. FOR MAY 1917.

2ⁿᵈ LONDON SANITARY COMPANY. R.A.M.C.T.

No. 12. SECTION.

1916. 3ʳᵈ CAVALRY DIVISION.

140/2/60

COMMITTEE FOR THE
MEDICAL HISTORY OF THE WAR
Date 10 JUL. 1917

WAR DIARY
or
INTELLIGENCE SUMMARY.
(Erase heading not required.)

Army Form C. 2118.

SANITARY SECTION
THIRD CAVALRY DIV.

Instructions regarding War Diaries and Intelligence Summaries are contained in F. S. Regs., Part II. and the Staff Manual respectively. Title pages will be prepared in manuscript.

Place	Date	Hour	Summary of Events and Information	Remarks and references to Appendices
Estaples	1st May		Inspection of sanitary arrangements of 7th L.A.M. Battery and 10th Reserve Park. Long pitched roof from Harlin for the Eveler which is working at 3 ovenfuls.	A.T.
La petit Moneyset le Bellechein	2nd		Arranged with 6th C.A. Brigade to run the Estaves when the 7th Brigade are disinfested. Saw ? came B.C.S.M. of the Leicester Yeomanry.	A.T.
Rouge Maison	3rd		Inspected sanitation of 7th M.G. Squadron and V6 battery.	A.T.
Epinoville	4th		Recest sprayed with cresol after ? diphtheria case had gone to hospital.	A.T.
Ronquet site.	4th		Delivered two disinfectors to 7th C.F.A. The Evelev went to the 7th M.G. Squadron. All wassers-traps were sprayed with dilute cresol 5%, but there were no striking differences in the flies on the places near treated to those in any case.	A.T.
Etaples			Went to see the M.O. i/c Laboratory about the suspected C.S.M. cases of the Leicester Yeo. There were definitely meningitis but no organisms recovered in the C.S. fluid.	A.T.
Auxmilles 6th			Inspected sanitation billets &c. of Ammunition Park and our horse transport. Examined clinical ? measles relapsed and those measles Evolu is working with 6th Brigade.	A.T.
Mainlery				A.T.

Army Form C. 2118.

WAR DIARY
or
INTELLIGENCE SUMMARY.
(Erase heading not required.)

Instructions regarding War Diaries and Intelligence
Summaries are contained in F. S. Regs., Part II.
and the Staff Manual respectively. Title pages
will be prepared in manuscript.

Place	Date	Hour	Summary of Events and Information	Remarks and references to Appendices
Division de Petit Chemin.	7th.		Inspected sanitation of billets, cookhouses, and water cart.	M.T.
Ammunt.	8th.		Inspected C. Battery, watercart.	A.T.
Bois Jean			Inspected B. Camp Gormany, water cart N.	
Maintenay			Inspected cart of 6 Cdn. C.F.A.	
Dominier			Cart .. 2nd Life Guards	
Tortefontaine			" .. cart .. 7th C.F.A.	
Dompierre			" .. cart .. 1st Life Guards	M.T.
Newpoulon	9th.		Notice boards for wells delivered to 7th C.F.A. & cert. for Fosse at Dominiersee.	
Maintenay Grand Preure			Fosse disinfecting N. Essuent germany.	
			B. received water cart to 2nd Dragon Guards at Grand Preure.	
Chelers d. Rouelt			8 Cd. C.F.A.	
Lepinang			8 Cd. N.C.C.S.	
Beauvoir villers			Supply Column	
Auchin Ct Vaant			10th Hussars.	A.T.

WAR DIARY
or
INTELLIGENCE SUMMARY.
(Erase heading not required.)

Army Form C. 2118.

Instructions regarding War Diaries and Intelligence Summaries are contained in F. S. Regs., Part II. and the Staff Manual respectively. Title pages will be prepared in manuscript.

Place	Date	Hour	Summary of Events and Information	Remarks and references to Appendices
Newport Brain	10th		Orders distributed North Command yeomanry.	NT
Tilgetani	11th		Long uneventful trive to D.A.S. 67 rapid & some patients to D.Stephens.	NT
Rouzgue	12th		Routine.	NT
Warara	13th		Moved to Warara by any road not arriving there before 4 pm.	NT
Tincourt	14th		Received orders to report to O.C. 4 & 8 Sanitary Section at inant with C.O.Ro O.C. 4 & 8 Sanitary Section were away on leave. Q officer had known nothing.	NT
Peronne	15th		Had Wire typho put to the Army. Endeavoured to find whether there was a definite even bespensive imputie of that received by the division or of military ottermed to know anything and was unable to communicate with the 3rd Cav Div.	NT
Tincourt	16th		Received of the 3rd Field Squadron R.E. at Roisin who had to afford out the Camp sites and already dug latrines etc. Fixed water provisional latid wells at Roisin & Tincourt. It has important that neither the Engineers nor J himself Staff we were told have been important. I am of a great and cautionary wood whisks pm the comps.	NT

WAR DIARY or INTELLIGENCE SUMMARY

Army Form C. 2118.

(Erase heading not required.)

Instructions regarding War Diaries and Intelligence Summaries are contained in F.S. Regs., Part II. and the Staff Manual respectively. Title pages will be prepared in manuscript.

Place	Date	Hour	Summary of Events and Information	Remarks and references to Appendices
Tincourt	17th		Spent the day going round the camps. Asked the A.D.M.S. Cavalry Corps if 9 was Brigade in a difficult area or not. He did not know. Long continued cooking for not Field Squadron.	D.T.
Cartelle			The will be installed of proud govt. (incorp. mp3) notice considered.	
Tincourt	18th		The men of this unit have been assisting in the construction of incinerators, refuse extrication one hundred as for will, saturating lattice brush for will etc.	
"	19th		The division moved in with everything half done. No latrines at had been completed. D.A.D.M.S. Car Corps did not know what villages 9 were reformed & refereeing.	M.T.
"	20th		Arranged for Manuor the latrine the camps so far as possible. Attended Conference on sanitation at Cav. Corps H.Q., a surprise attends to come. Nr Norman obtained for straight-lines & plan site of corps rest station	A.T.
Catelet				
T–court	21st		Moved the workshop & the aid medical by so Sanitary Section.	A.T.
Tincourt	22nd		Inspectors not out having allotted when returning at night.	
			Inspected latrine wells etc at opening and Templeux-la-Fosse.	A.T.
"	23rd		Drew lorries from Persan Carter & arranged for now the best medical Carter since working so rooms. The XIIth tripod manure dumps uncovered	

WAR DIARY
or
INTELLIGENCE SUMMARY.
(Erase heading not required.)

Army Form C. 2118.

[Stamp: SANITARY SECTION, THIRD CAVALRY DIV.]

Place	Date	Hour	Summary of Events and Information	Remarks and references to Appendices
Tuserval	23rd		with Major Lecesne Q. in order said manure was to be dumped. I asked for it to be burnt and between the two nothing was done. It was put down on the ground & let alone practically. Invited latrines, grease traps, ablutions etc. made is workshops and put up aunng this week.	A.T.
	24th		Saw trouble with 8th brigade over having horses with 7th brigade. Begged S.O. Coment dinner at Pernes and showed how round Moiret Cantien. Workshops kept busy all day. Model field oven built.	A.T.
	25th		almost all detached men have returned to their units. One is charged again to that occupied by the division only. Forward a note asking of several attendants of time at for emergency, latrines and shelters and extra pots to promise. Began the construction of 20 Phypereut seats for the sickdown latrines in the Trenches.	A.T.
	26th		Workshops turned out latrine notes towards the on part as promised. Rather were taken over in the village from Lee Sanitary Section. Obtained list of milk supplier requiring testing from Q. and went over to Eps	A.T.
Eps				

2353 W1 W 2544/1454 700,000 5/15 D.D.&L. A.D.S.S./Forms/C. 2118.

WAR DIARY
or
INTELLIGENCE SUMMARY.

Army Form C. 2118.

Place	Date	Hour	Summary of Events and Information	Remarks and references to Appendices
Turcoint	24th		samples in bottles for the railway traverdre tent. These will be taken in from had in every bomb reserve which worked twice and the Epithy who were not knocked out worked. Two P.R. were again hospitalised later.	AT
"	3 p.m.		Two O.Rs who had been out to Contigny from Doingt by the train began there and all were outside my mess, came back the same day a aching. Two O.R. reinforcements arrived.	
			The hostility report was printed and it took the clerk & myself all day to look out the previous correctly. It appears the wound to consolidated for any unspf and there is much repetition. I certainly want a practical system ceded water at Epithy again and found pits loads to town.	AT
Epithy	28th		Spoke to O.P.S. 6th Brigade and arranged that it was both possible and easy for the waste food remnants etc from the grew lines to be sent up in sacks to the ration dump by them going by its rations and carried back by the empty wagons returning to Villers-Faucon.	AT
Ti no N Pyth.			Two O. Rs attached to Our Major Villers-Faucon and one to Town Major Epithy as inspectors etc.	

WAR DIARY or INTELLIGENCE SUMMARY

Army Form C. 2118.

Place	Date	Hour	Summary of Events and Information	Remarks and references to Appendices
Tincourt	30th Sept. 3rd		Inspected Sanitation of but life grounds, also cooks at Tincourt, Buire etc. Erected manure incinerators & chaffed piece of corrugated iron. Drew some wood & tarred iron from the R.E. dump at Peziel.	Nil
			During the month three O.Rs have been inspecting the horse lines & camps of the three brigades and returning everynight with reports of any sanitary items. O.Rs are detailed on duty keeping the Town drains of Villers Faucon, Doingt & Epeshy as these villages are kept for daily visits. One O.R. is creosoting wells and watercarts daily. Three carpenters are at work and two plumbers in the workshops Two O.Rs are in charge of the baths and the others help in the workshop innovations and the fitting up of latrines made in the workshops. Drain pattern by Foden. Mileage 42½ Artistes 3434 Coal one Ton	

Army Form C. 2118.

WAR DIARY
or
INTELLIGENCE SUMMARY.
(Erase heading not required.)

Instructions regarding War Diaries and Intelligence Summaries are contained in F.S. Regs., Part II. and the Staff Manual respectively. Title pages will be prepared in manuscript.

Place	Date	Hour	Summary of Events and Information	Remarks and references to Appendices
Tidworth			Summary of work done in week ending present Form water latrines .... 4 Three " .... 2 Two " .... 1 One " .... 5 Fly proof lids for latrines repaired/new 12 Latrine fly traps repaired/or furnished 20 and 10 still in stock Native brands revision 12 Ventilating shafts for A.D.S. dug outs 2 Soap racks for baths 20 pair. Duck boarding for baths 4710 square feet. No. of waters tested 28 " Watercarts 14 In hands not yet finished two new water latrines M R Hampton Capt O.C.	

WAR DIARY FOR MAY. 1917

No. 12 Sanitary Section. 2nd London Sanitary Company, R.A.M.C. T.
3rd CAVALRY DIVISION.

WAR DIARY
for
No. 12 SANITARY SECTION

June 1917.
2ⁿᵈ LONDON SANITARY Co: R.A.M.C. T.

JUNE 1917.

140/2231

COMMITTEE FOR THE
MEDICAL HISTORY OF THE WAR
Date -7 AUG 1917

Army Form C. 2118.

WAR DIARY
or
INTELLIGENCE SUMMARY.
(Erase heading not required.)

June 1917

Instructions regarding War Diaries and Intelligence Summaries are contained in F. S. Regs., Part II. and the Staff Manual respectively. Title pages will be prepared in manuscript.

SANITARY SECTION
THIRD CAVALRY DIV.

Place	Date	Hour	Summary of Events and Information	Remarks and references to Appendices
Tincourt	1st		General montris.	
Epehy			Site chosen for spray bathes. Went to inspect for two dugouts of A.D.S.	A.F.
Tincourt	2nd		Motor lorries in circular patrols. Transport made with Q for spray baths.	
Buire	3rd		Site chosen for spray baths & plans of baths have given G.R.E.	
			Incinerator improved for 7th Brigade.	
Tincourt	4th		Suspected latrine obtained 6 3rd L.C., Trench latrines for D sector. 5 latrine platforms	A.F.
			& R.H.G. made. Water samples taken from wells at Epehy, & mobile beyond Rd. Porrine.	
Buire	5th		Two cases ? dysentery from 10th R. Dragons. No none ? Gorge from both men isolated.	A.F.
			Urine taken from both troops. Instruction to watch for hens & eat of 6 E & F 7th Brigades. Not	
			Trench latrines started for 7th Brigade HQrs. Three peril latrine lines. Germany finished in	
			boarty of wells, incinerators of & prisat of Longavesne.	
Tincourt	6th		Supply of well water taken at Epehy for R.E. encouraged to Porrine. Antiviral latrine cleaning	
			system for bathers at Epehy. Instrn neut te 6 3rd C.F.A. Firm order latrine into standard at	A.F.
			13th Colonel battalion Doingt. Water instruction given to 7th Brigade into duty men.	
Tincourt	7th		Pay wines summer bar given to Corpt A.G. Many water eta measured at wells tank at	
			Tincourt. 19 drum latrines sent for the troops. Water samples troops/horts Porrine.	A.F.

2333 W: W: 2514/1454. 700,000. 5/15. D. D. & L. A.D.S.S./Forms/C. 2118.

Army Form C. 2118.

WAR DIARY
or
INTELLIGENCE SUMMARY.
(Erase heading not required.)

Instructions regarding War Diaries and Intelligence Summaries are contained in F. S. Regs., Part II. and the Staff Manual respectively. Title pages will be prepared in manuscript.

Place	Date	Hour	Summary of Events and Information	Remarks and references to Appendices
Trinon N.	7th.		Both ADMS & ODMS. asked for report on the units supplying their troops & apparent content.	A.E.
Trinon N.	8th.		Inspected all manure dumps & the incinerators in the division. All appears satisfactory. I.O.R. inspected the billeting of the cavalry troops located in Brion. Trinken down latrines were noted.	A.E.
Trinon V.	9th. 10th.		Supervision of confirmed of Brion continued. Conveyance of material for R.E. for this purpose. Hay the unit visited the 4th Army ordered of Sanitation & Provencale. All known incinerators again inspected. Several inspections made to form Major & Plots of the purpose sanitation there. Located latrines replaced satisfactorily.	A.E.
Trinon V.	11th.		Advised 6 C.B. 7th & 8th Brigades where typre bathing parade in river. They were instructed to obtain met & Saulcourt. 3 O.Rs. enteric & B.E. at Brion latter.	A.E.
Trinon V.	12th.		All wells inspected at Villers Faucon in this area. Two of his troops for mules pissed out. Cardless used at Saulcourt.	M.E.
Trinon V.	13th.		Inspected manure incinerators in division, endeavored to have service & care of same explained to 2Lt. M.O.s of squadrons.	M.E.

Army Form C. 2118.

WAR DIARY
or
INTELLIGENCE SUMMARY.
(Erase heading not required.)

Instructions regarding War Diaries and Intelligence Summaries are contained in F. S. Regs., Part II. and the Staff Manual respectively. Title pages will be prepared in manuscript.

Place	Date	Hour	Summary of Events and Information	Remarks and references to Appendices
Tinicourt	14th		Made first billeting arrangements for 6th & 7th Cav. Brigades with Q. Brigade joined with two brigades next to 7th Cav. Brigade. Two tanks proceeded to ADSS Latrine with std. 2nd L.G. nets.	AT
Tinicourt M.	15th		Approved of O.C. Sanitary section decided, Corps H.Q. This appears n'west of Etrier. Two forward latrines with stands to Ecavy Infantry. Baths at Morion were opened.	AT
"	16th		Inspected all units at Doingt. Admired clustering of ? 0730 unit of Infantry & etc. painted no unpaired water troughs in dewing the streams. 12 drum latrine next to 2 Sections. Boiler of Tinicourt baths dismantled cleaned & repaired.	AT
	17th		Inspected Ammuting at Tinicourt which hampered three quadrant chevrons of bins near a luminous. Admired removed to more suitable site & attention of medical of mound.	AT
	18th		Inspected faults of Villers Faucon. Running lavatory unit units late Army return functions. Inspected manure incinerators. Admired made some improving indications to the crater at Funcillers. Erected Latrines with stand appointed to shot heavy battery R.E.A. at Villers Faucon.	AT
"	19th		W. latrines inspected & restored. Officer latrines erected Tinicourt M. Two units here brought in water erected at Villers Faucon.	AT

2353 Wt. W2544/1454 700,000 5/15 D.D.&L. A.D.S.S./Form/C. 2118.

WAR DIARY
or Intelligence
INTELLIGENCE SUMMARY.

Army Form C. 2118.

(Erase heading not required.)

Instructions regarding War Diaries and Intelligence Summaries are contained in F. S. Regs., Part II. and the Staff Manual respectively. Title pages will be prepared in manuscript.

SANITARY SECTION — THIRD CAVALRY DIV.

Place	Date	Hour	Summary of Events and Information	Remarks and references to Appendices
Tincourt	20th		Appearance of troops when exactly the same, groundings, press, no as before. Weather better, a slight southerly wind.	AT
"	21st		Accompanied A.D.M.S. inspecting 7th C. Brigade Camp. Billets to be multiplied straight. Water at Cavalier inspected. Scarp brewery & billets troops evacuated at Bernes Cattle Mousetrap for Cavalier food in troops.	AT
"	22nd		Pump well in ruins at Epéhy. The importance of the wells supplied by A.D.M.S. orders were wrong so the troops troubles with prisoners in that some of them could be poisoned. On this occasion I accompanied Lt. Col. Epéhy & Settle Mon. Francois. Acted the R. Est. verify the appearance troops will be SANITARE in order. That complying water from wells at Petit Revel Ferme & Pigeon Ravine & Prisoner for examination. A letter from the A.D.T. Cavaliers sent.	AT
"	23rd			
"	24th		Notice board erected at Bernes.	AT
"	25th		Inspection of 8th cav. Brigade. Notice boards erected at Saulcourt.	AT
"	26th		Hospital returns of 3rd D. Cavalier. a new country gets taken up, inter as with AT.	
			The same troubles happens as there is no disparity, alarm checked. Used with the AC C. R. U. to the Army H. Q. & the D.M.S. as arranging for care of hospital to dust drawing 3 army as before.	AT

Army Form C. 2118.

WAR DIARY
for June 1917
INTELLIGENCE SUMMARY.
(Erase heading not required.)

Instructions regarding War Diaries and Intelligence Summaries are contained in F.S. Regs., Part II. and the Staff Manual respectively. Title pages will be prepared in manuscript.

Place	Date	Hour	Summary of Events and Information	Remarks and references to Appendices
Tincourt	27th		A dental conference took up H.Q. 18 down letters taken to Division. Water samples were still much by R.E. Spade for were dug the earth was notified. Application was made for another lorry to move the with out the hand. This was reported that these were who have no bicycle must go by train.	AF
"	28th			AF
"	29th		All men were recalled from Leinct. Eply & Villers Faucon in accordance with instructions from D.D.M.S. (telephonic) and the one in the hospital was promptly to a Sanitary Section. The lorouts for the wounded walls at Eply was vacated. The weekly report was returned to be amended as it was too long etc. last month. It was too full.	AF
"	30th		Boards were erected over the to wells in the area of Tincourt. Revised lists of wells in the area printed and sent to A.D.M.S.	AF

2353 Wt. W2544/1454 700,000 9/15 D.D.&L. A.D.S.S./Forms/C. 2118.

WAR DIARY
for June
INTELLIGENCE SUMMARY.
(Erase heading not required.)

Army Form C. 2118.

Place	Date	Hour	Summary of Events and Information	Remarks and references to Appendices
Thierin N	30th.		The present composition of a new Sany section strips all the men of the unit to work. This is natural for infantry but it is impossible to keep up with cavalry as the length of a days march is often too much in proportion of say from the average speed of cavalry being 5 m.p.h. Some extra transport is needed for mon Sany sections attached to cavalry division. The area has been divided up between the sanitary inspectors, and where there never have been before, proximity roads from the nature sect bought, villus Farnew & B. pithy the inspectors have been attached to the town mayors. Four O.Rs have been working in the carpenters shop. One O.R. has been testing wells and priming up heads for them. Three O.R. have been in charge of baths assisted by two P.B. men. The remainder assist in the workshops etc & in erecting the appliances made there.	

A.C.C. Thompson
Capt.
o/c 12th Sanitary Section.

www.ingramcontent.com/pod-product-compliance
Lightning Source LLC
Chambersburg PA
CBHW080849230426
43662CB00013B/2057